MINNIE GASTEL

Translated by Frederika Randall

The Versace Legend

Baldini Castoldi Dalai
Publishers since 1897

www.bcdeditions.com

Original Title: Il mito Versace

Copyright © Baldini Castoldi Dalai *editore* S.p.A. - Milano, 2007.
© 2008 Baldini Castoldi Dalai *editore* Inc.
ISBN 978-88-6073-427-3
Library of Congress Cataloging-in-Publication
Information is available from the Library of Congress
upon request.

Printed and bound in Italy by
Grafica Veneta S.p.A. - Trebaseleghe (PD)

To Guido, Giovanni and Francesco

Contents

My warmest gratitude goes to Flora Casalinuovo, who proved an indispensable assistant.

My sincere thanks, too, to Fiammetta Roditi, director of MODAcontents/Tremelloni (Dipartimento Indaco) Politeca at the Milan Politecnico, along with all her staff.

Thanks also to Patrizia Cucco, who worked closely with Gianni Versace and serves as his in-house memory, and who, with great courtesy and precision, let me in on the extraordinary professional adventure she shared with him.

M.G.

I am a tailor, a dressmaker. When I first arrived in Milan from Reggio Calabria, I had to forget all that I had learned from my mother, because I found there was another language, other techniques. Then slowly, I realized that what she had taught me was still good. I learned that the true artist is an artisan. It makes me laugh when certain designers say they are not dressmakers, not tailors. Certainly, if you look at their clothes, that's evident. As I see it, the true artist is one who makes things with his own hands. A designer, therefore, must be a dressmaker.

Gianni Versace, 1990

CHAPTER 1
Beginnings

Reggio Calabria, southern Italy, the early 1950s.

All the stylish ladies in the city of Reggio Calabria had their clothes made by Franca Versace. She was the top dressmaker in town, and in fact in the whole of Calabria. No one was as good as she was. In the 1950s the fashion that mattered was Paris haute couture, and Italian dressmakers bought paper patterns from Dior, Givenchy and Balenciaga and faithfully reproduced them to make fashionable clothes for their clients. But Franca Versace didn't merely follow the patterns. She was too much her own person to copy from someone else, even when that someone was one of the Olympic deities of fashion. As a girl, she had wanted to study medicine, but her father thought the profession was too masculine. So she had studied dressmaking with "La Parigina," the best in town. Franca—who was baptized Francesca but preferred the snappier, stronger and more definitive Franca—got her inspiration from the French designers, but as soon as she began to cut her fabric—i.e., right away—she would start to modify the line with bursts of creativity that made it almost impossible to tell who was the original couturier.

Her husband, Antonio, was a wholesale and retail coal merchant, but above all he loved books, poetry and the opera. Franca dearly loved all three of her children: Tina, born November 10, 1943; Santo, born December 16, 1944; and Gianni, born December 2, 1946. (Donatella would come along on May 2, 1955.) But she had a special feeling for Gianni, a deep affinity. After school Gianni didn't play with toy cars but preferred to hide behind the curtain in his mother's shop and watch her clients try on their dresses. Anna Lucritano, Lilli Condello, Pina Liconti, Signora Nunnari and all the rest of the wives of the most prosperous businessmen and professionals of Reggio Calabria. Ladies who would show off their clothes at society parties, extravagant weddings and during the *struscio* when they strolled down the streets of the town center. Later, when he had become famous, Gianni never tired of his warm and happy memories of those days.

"I've often talked about that long-ago time of my childhood, a time that may sound mythical, made-up and unreal," he told journalist Roberto Alessi and fashion historian Nicoletta Bocca. "But it really is true: I can still remember the smells of the dressmaking shop, I can see the colors, the red of the curtain behind which I, a child of six, no more, was hidden. I remember the black velvet dress, extremely elegant, that my mother was fitting on a client, Signora Ippolito. I can see my mother's hands. I can almost see the client being transformed under her touch, as if some magic were being performed. I thought: Now my mother's going to shorten the dress in front and leave it longer behind, and then she's going to do something that breaks the rules, something daring. And it would happen, just as I imagined. Even though I was still so small, something was already decided in me. That fitting, as it turns out, has never really come to an end. And that black dress, so hieratic, is still there: the first dress I can remember." That black dress would become a kind of touchstone for Versace the designer; he would make it and remake it, collection after collection, adjusting it to the times, whether long and sleek with the décolleté of an evening dress, or short and sweet. He called it his "memory dress."

Gianni's relationship with his mother was instinctive and profound. With his father, Antonio, things were more difficult. Yet they too had something in common. Antonio was a merchant but he loved art and the opera. He could recite verses from *The Iliad* and *The Odyssey* from memory. When Gianni was only a few years old his father took him for the first time to the Cilea Theater of Reggio Calabria to see Verdi's *Ballo in maschera*. Too small to follow the story, Gianni was nevertheless enchanted by the singers in their marvelous costumes and by the excitement in the foyer. His father also took him to the movies: to see Silvana Mangano in *Riso amaro*, and Sophia Loren and Gina Lollobrigida. Performance, entertainment—they had an instinctive attraction for him. One of his favorite pastimes was to dress puppets with scraps of cloth from his mother's shop and make them perform on his own little stage.

Ordinary life outside the shop interested him less. He was not very enthusiastic about his high school classes. He was always half-distracted, always drawing fashion sketches in his notebooks. One teacher summoned his mother in alarm and told her of his habit—to the teacher practically a perversion. To the teacher those drawings had something pornographic about them, something provocative, something morbid. In fact, little Gianni was merely trying to copy the beautiful, sexy actresses he had seen at the movies. Franca Versace reassured the teacher, but she also understood that academic studies were not for her son. She didn't however send him, as he would have liked, to the conservatory, but decided she preferred a more traditional, if not very ambitious, credential. Gianni would get a diploma as a *geometra,* a draftsman-surveyor. It's hard to imagine anything further from Gianni's DNA than this petit bourgeois profession, one that the boy, in fact, never pursued.

No, Gianni was much more at his ease looking at the sea out the family window, the sea which at that point on the Strait,[1] looks like a lake. He could see, close up, the palms and the cathedral, and beneath them, the mosaics of the Roman baths with their figures of dolphins and the Medusa in blue and Pompeiian red. Gianni was also happy when he vacationed on the Ionian and at Santo Stefano d'Aspromonte, where you could walk in the woods without meeting another soul and breathe in the enchanting solitude. And naturally Gianni was perfectly at his ease in his mother's dressmaking shop, where he quickly became her most valuable assistant. He was just

---

1. Reggio Calabria sits on the Strait of Messina across from the island of Sicily.

over 20 years old when Franca sent him out as a buyer for the two boutiques in Reggio, one selling women's fashions and one men's. Gianni began to travel to Rome, to Milan, to Paris, to London. It was the end of the 1960s, and Paris was the realm of Pierre Cardin, of the modernist Paco Rabanne with his tiny dresses of plastic and metal chips, and of Karl Lagerfeld who was relaunching Chloé. Swinging London had its young, nonconformist look by Biba, its miniskirts by Mary Quant and its razor-thin models Jean Shrimpton and Twiggy. For Gianni Versace, a world was opening up.

Santo, two years older, was his father's favorite. At 18, he had enrolled at the University of Messina to study business administration and economics while continuing to help his father with his business. Gianni wasn't jealous of Santo, who was protective of his younger brother. "He was my victim," Gianni said as an adult. "I could twist him around my little finger. I would get him to give me money because I knew he could always go to our father for more." Santo was a real older brother; he shared the tastes of his father, a man who had competed several times in the Giro d'Italia bike race and played soccer with the Reggina C team. He even had the family's political passion: his grandfather, a shoemaker, had been a friend of Matteotti,[2] and whenever a Fascist official had come to town, the grandfather had been taken off to jail for a couple of days to keep him out of trouble. Santo himself

---

2. Socialist MP Giacomo Matteotti was murdered by the Fascists in 1924.

would join the Socialist federation in Reggio. And even as a child, he was always the balanced brother, the one who looked after people, who followed society's rules and built himself a future based on education and sports. In his free time, Santo played basketball. Carlo Casile, a childhood friend interviewed by Mario Guarino, recalls that he was a strong player and became captain of the Reggio basketball team, the Aics (later called Piero Viola). Santo never forgot his team, and in 1998 helped out when the team was in financial straits, because he had fond memories and because he was convinced that "basketball, one of the most beautiful sports in existence," was "all-important for Reggio Calabria."

Santo was the wise man of the family. Here's how he remembers his father: "He taught me the meaning of work, as a duty first, a right second, although he always left me free to choose my field of operation. My father was the only one who said nothing when I left a secure job at Credito Italiano bank to work for myself as a tax accountant." And Antonio confirmed Santo's special role in the family; the father who was so taciturn and distant made Santo's favored position explicit for the first time during a Christmas celebration in the mid-1980s in the fabulous villa at Moltrasio on Lake Como that Gianni had bought and renovated in 1980. In one of those family reunions dear to southern Italian tradition for which Gianni had a special soft spot, the family talked about work, about problems, about their plans. At a certain point Donatella turned to her father: "Papà...." She went no further because Antonio interrupted and nodding at Santo said, "You need to speak to him." When Gianni began his career as a designer, Santo was behind him, studying the first contracts with the big fashion houses. And he was there beside his talented and creative younger sibling—Santo, the big brother who knew about business—when it came time to register the brand and the company in 1977.

Besides Santo and Gianni there was Tina, their sister who sadly, at ten years of age, contracted peritonitis and died. Gianni never forgot his mother's desperation in those dramatic days. "She seemed to have lost her mind. She was there day and night with my sister; I had been sent to my aunt and uncle's. But I was terribly upset. One morning I ran away and went home. As I came in, I saw the lifeless body of my sister in the open casket with masses of white flowers around her. I felt I couldn't breathe. I went up to my mother, who was kneeling by the casket, and took her hand. 'Tina has gone to heaven,' she told me, weeping. 'Now I only have you and Santo.' " For a long time, the mood in the family was bitterly sad. Franca Versace had changed; she was unable to work and often she cried, although she tried to hide her sadness. "And then one day," Gianni recalled, "she said to me, 'Gianni, soon you're going to have another little sister.' "

On May 2, 1955, Donatella was born. She was not merely the youngest in the family but she came as a reminder of Tina, so she began life with an advantage and she was destined to be protected, cared-for and spoiled. Nine years divided Gianni and his sister, but right away they developed a very strong bond. "Gianni and I had the same character, the same personality," Donatella told

Jacaranda Falck in an article in the news magazine *L'Espresso*. "Santo, luckily, is different from us, he's more even-tempered, more rational." The first clothes that Gianni cut were for Donatella. When she turned ten, Gianni advised her to put blond highlights in her hair. Donatella wore the first fashions with the Versace label. She recalled two key moments in their early days together, when she was only a few years old. "Gianni trusted me with an important duty," she told Giusy Ferré. "I was supposed to warn him when my parents were coming so they wouldn't find him playing. Another time, seeing that I had proved myself trustworthy, Gianni asked me to get the car keys that were lying on the bedside table beside Mamma and Papà's bed. He wanted to go out and listen to music while the rest of us were sleeping. Most children will try to find a way not to obey the orders of an older brother. But that never happened with us, because everything he asked me to do seemed like fun. I've never met anyone who was more exciting, more capable of surprising me with every move he made." If there hadn't been this inborn complicity, there never would have been that implicit understanding between Gianni and Donatella that began when Gianni first sought out Donatella's opinion and treated her something like his muse, and that later became an unrivaled personal and professional harmony. Drawn by the world of fashion, enchanted by her brother's genius, Donatella would abandon her studies in literature at the University of Florence to become first Gianni's shadow and later his right hand.

CHAPTER 2
From Reggio Calabria to Milan

Young Gianni Versace was ready to take another step on his journey. In February 1972 he moved to Tuscany, between Lucca and Florence. He would arrive in Milan in November of the same year, moving into the Principessa Clothilde Residence in the Porta Nuova district. His one large room was full of books and magazines and looked more like a student's quarters than the workshop of a fashion designer. Then he moved to Via della Spiga 2, and after that into another wonderful apartment in Via Melegari, near Corso Venezia, in an elegant, secluded neighborhood of early 20th-century townhouses inhabited by the Milanese moneyed class. There, in Via Cappuccini, Enrica Invernizzi kept herons, deer and peacocks in her opulent garden. Gianni was 25 years old. He had come to Milan to keep an eye on the collection that Enzo Nicosia and Salvatore Chiodini, proprietors of Florentine Flowers, a knitwear house in Lucca, had asked him to design. The two textile entrepreneurs sensed there was something urgent and new developing in their business.

The Sala Bianca at Palazzo Pitti in Florence was then the elegant showcase for Italian fashion. A far-sighted

Florentine, Marchese Giovanni Battista Giorgini, had persuaded the first Italian fashion houses—Marucelli, Veneziani, Emilio Pucci—to show their collections there amid the gold leaf and plaster of Palazzo Pitti. On this magnificent and urbane stage, he had introduced journalists and international buyers to the crème de la crème of native fashion, which was just then beginning to produce its first collections and compete with Paris couture. Twenty years later, however, when Versace arrived, times had changed—and then some. The tsunami effect of 1968 had dragged Italy into another epoch, and the world of fashion reflected the changes in taste and mentality. There were miniskirts, the new symbols of women's emancipation; there was folk, with its hints of alternative cultures; there was "flower power" and its echoes of the newborn peace movement. New ideas and striking new looks were in. The two textile manufacturers from Lucca understood that Gianni Versace had the magic touch that could rejuvenate their line and make it sparkle. And Versace himself was already fairly confident about his own talent. So he called Walter Albini, a leading designer of the moment with whom he had become friends, and asked him how much he was getting paid for a collection. Four million lire, Albini told him, so Gianni too asked for four million. And Nicosia and Chiodini gave it to him, along with a smashing premium, a black VW Beetle convertible with a white roof.

At first Gianni made them a little nervous. Although he knew virtually nothing about knitwear, he had a very clear idea of how he wanted the collection to look, with lavish, complicated patterns, things like cables and stitches on the bias, that had never been done before. Since he didn't know anything about the technical specifications for knitted fabrics, he simply treated the material as if it were woven. And Nicosia and Chiodini gave him a free hand. With that flexibility so characteristic of Italian artisans, they were happy to permit him to experiment with new patterns. And people liked Gianni's work, so much so that soon he heard from another fashion entrepreneur, Gigi Monti. Along with Aldo Ferrante and Gianni Tositti, Monti owned FTM, a company that sold designer styles, and counted among its clients Franca Versace. Gianni had long accompanied his mother to visit Monti and buy fashions for the Reggio Calabria boutique. Now Monti asked Gianni to work on some designs for FTM.

Through Monti, Gianni met Giuseppe Menta, a fabric designer. To the sophisticated Menta, then keen on Russian constructivist art, Gianni proposed two print patterns: one of roses overlaid on woven straw, and one of swallows and music scores. Menta recalls the young man with affection. "His ideas were ingenuous, innocent, a bit too fifties. But I produced them anyway, even though I knew they wouldn't work. I took them to FTM and then I told Gianni he ought to aim at something different. He was very smart and very eager to learn, and he did. I saw that he was really keen to work, and had extraordinary energy. And from that time on, between Gianni—who would go on to become what he became—and myself, a fascinating partnership grew up that lasted until his death in 1997." Menta also recalls another episode: "I brought him a bolt of cloth with longitudinal stripes, stripes that would stop and then start up again where the cloth was supposed to be cut. Gianni paid no attention, taking the fabric and draping on the dummy, so that where the stripes broke off, they made a decorative pattern on the bias. So you see, he was able to profit from a mistake and make something come out of it!"

In the evenings, Menta used to go to a hangout called the Osteria dei Binari, where the smart Milan design world went to listen to Gerry Mulligan and his jazz. He took Versace with him, and there Gianni met textile producer Fabio Bellotti and Ugo Correani, who became his right hand man for accessories. "I wanted to introduce him to the fashion world," Menta recalls, "and Gianni was pleased to have the opportunity, even though he participated in his own particular way, somewhat shyly, intent mostly on what could be useful to him in his work." Around this time, the young Calabrian designer took advantage of a golden opportunity. The Callaghan Group out of Novara, which produced avant-garde clothes and knitwear, lost its in-house genius Walter Albini. Famous for his style based on French period chic of the teens, twenties and thirties, Albini's name was attached to an exclusive line produced by Callaghan. "We already knew Gianni," says Marisa Zanetti Greppi, the founder of Callaghan, "because he came to us for clothes and fabrics for the Reggio Calabria boutique. When Albini left, a couple of colleagues suggested Gianni. And so one morning he arrived here with his briefcase to order fabrics for his mother, and by that evening when he left our offices, he had a contract with us as a designer. It was always a pleasure to work with him; he was tireless, precise, generous and easy to get along with. Right away, he brought with him a breath of fresh air, revolutionizing and speeding up the design process. At first he had to adapt himself and stick close to Albini's style, because that was what clients wanted. Then one day he just exploded."

Here Marisa, today a youthful-looking 70 years old, momentarily betrays her emotion. "He became more confident, he began to express himself. The real Versace appeared, and he was a triumph. The fact is, Gianni revolutionized fashion. Before him, clothes were sober, bourgeois, often boring. Gianni added color, he began to mix his fabrics and use unusual materials, he tried out a sexy décolleté here and a form-fitting skirt there. He wanted his women to be *beautiful*." Moved by her memories, she goes on: "He was a workhorse, a flood of inspiration. He arrived in the office, took off his jacket and rolled up his sleeves. He would go into the warehouse and get the fabrics. He'd bring them into his atelier and begin to work straight-away on the dummy. He would cut, stitch, drape and remake the model. Often he'd take off his shoes to be more comfortable, and I'd follow him around to keep him from stepping on the dozens of pins that lay on the floor. He could go on like that for hours, until he achieved perfection. He always had a notebook with him, because wherever he was, whenever, he might start to sketch something he had in mind, and his thoughts flowed even faster than his pencil. He relied on his own judgment, but at the same time, he always wanted to hear the opinions of his assistants. He was very open to dialogue, very available. And he had a lot of fun. He always had a smile on his face because he *loved* his work. We worked together for fourteen years, and they were Callaghan's best years, and the best years of my life."

In those same days, another opportunity presented itself. In 1974 Florentine Flowers, with its updated look, showed its collection in the Sala Bianca at Palazzo Pitti. Among the buyers present for the shows that year were Arnaldo and Donatella Girombelli, prosperous clothing manufacturers with a big factory in the central Italian city of Ancona. Their line was called Genny, after Arnaldo's firstborn—a line that had started out as a simple series of skirts and blouses but had branched out into a real collection. They were in search of an emerging designer who could give a fresh new look to the line. "Giuseppe Menta put us on to Florentine Flowers and Versace," Donatella Girombelli recalls. "He told me that the Versace designs he had seen had a rare glamour and femininity. And so we made an appointment with Gianni Versace. He was tall and pale-skinned with a dark beard, and despite the beard he looked like a boy out of his element. And in fact, he was still a novice at Palazzo Pitti. A few days later we met in Milan and signed the contract immediately. Versace told me that he had begun in his mother's dress shop and that he wanted to get into industrial prêt-à-porter. He was intelligent, very forward-thinking, and his ideas were very clear. Our connection began there and we worked together for many years, until

1992." Arnaldo Girombelli took care of the business side. Donatella followed the design side and marketing. She and Gianni quickly found themselves in tune with one other.

"He understood perfectly what the Genny woman should be: not high fashion, not terribly young, but very modern. He was terrific when it came to mixing fabrics. In a time when everyone was showing tailored suits for women, he mixed it up. He would take a Prince of Wales check jacket and put it with a pair of hazelnut brown pants, and underneath a silk blouse printed with roses. He loved contrasts, he was always mixing sporty and elegant. He would tack lace on top of a hound's-tooth check, stir up the various fantasies." In those years of the early 1970s, when the fashionable woman often looked androgynous, Versace offered a look that was sporty and modern, but also very feminine, "with a touch of poetry." Later, he would design for a woman who was less sweet, more aggressive.

Genny quickly became a famous brand. "Because," says Donatella Girombelli, "Gianni had a rare creative streak but he also had a strong commercial instinct. He was able to target the product perfectly." Gianni Bertasso, long-time fashion editor, in those days chief editor of *Giornale tessile*, which later became *Fashion* (and today *Mood*), remembers, "When Genny's eighteen suits came out, all of them were already sold. Gianni had created such an 'addiction' among his clients that women would reserve his clothes even before they appeared in the shops. The call would come in from the boutique carrying

Genny, 'We've got the new suits, shall I put the red one or the blue one away for you?' And that's how it was as long as he was the designer."

Versace, however, was anything but a smooth operator. When he began to design a collection, he generally had a clear idea of what he was up to. He sketched things out with a couple of pencil lines, then had the fabric brought to him, and he would touch it, take it in hand, drape it spectacularly, make it live. Only then did he put down a rudimentary drawing, which an artist would convert into a finished sketch. Then there was a first fitting with cloth, a second trial with a different fabric, then finally a further fitting with the definitive choice of fabric. And for every number, right from the start, Versace designed many variations. Everything could still change. Even his fashion shows changed right up to the last minute, and if the collection hadn't had to be sold, Versace would have gone on perpetually adjusting his designs. During the runway show, Gianni stayed backstage to dress the models—nervous and insecure, although he didn't show it. But when the exam was over, he would return to his cheerful, amusing self.

"We'd be up until three or four a.m. laughing," Donatella Girombelli recalls. "Gianni was charming, he was fun, he had a great thirst for knowledge. Every morning he bought about fifteen newspapers and magazines. He often stayed with us in Ancona, and we traveled a lot together, to St. Petersburg, to New York; we had a great friendship. He was a real professional, interested in everything. He did everything with passion and commitment, and he had great energy. His sister Donatella, who was studying in Florence, began to accompany him only when he started to design the Complice line. Gianni had a lot of confidence in his sister's judgment, even back then." At a certain point in 1977, Gianni put his name to three lines—Genny, Callaghan and Complice—the last the Girombelli's hip young collection, on which Gianni lavished stunning new colors he made up himself. He adored his work, but felt a great responsibility toward those who worked with him. "What if I fail?" he would agonize to Donatella Girombelli every time he turned out a collection. "Hundreds of people depend on me."

It was true, because prêt-à-porter—ready-to-wear—had become big business. Milan, following the boom years of the fifties and sixties, had become the locomotive of the national economy. In Milan, fashion designers met those who produced fashion and those who sold it. In this most efficient and business-minded of Italian cities, many clothing firms had opened their commercial offices and showrooms where they could display their fashions all year round, without any of the restrictions they had to deal with in Florence. The great wheel of fashion was moving in many dimensions; its prospects were opening up. Milan responded with the effervescence that always accompanies the new. The designers of the moment, nearly all of them destined to be stars—Albini, Ken Scott, Krizia, Missoni—carved their showrooms out of all kinds of spaces: theaters, cafés, private clubs, art galleries, circus tents. Versace was younger than the others, but he made his mark right away. *Vogue France* reported on the Rustica collection from Callaghan's fall-winter line-up for 1976–1977: "Versace gives the folk look a decidedly modern and dynamic interpretation. His style, full of youthful spirit, is beginning to give a distinctive look to Italian avant-garde fashion. Although he was almost unknown three years ago, today Versace is one of the most talked-about designers." And that was Paris talking. Not bad, Gianni.

"In search of his own original style, Gianni Versace has, in a very short time, already distanced himself from the crowd," wrote fashion historian Nicoletta Bocca. "His point of reference is no longer the European street fashion of 1968; he's drawing more and more on American youth culture, and particularly on the rock music and disco world, the movie world." Versace would never abandon this love for performance and show business; it would remain one of his strongest sources of inspiration. You can see it as early as the first collection that Gianni designed for Complice, in fall-winter 1977–1978. The collection was called "new romantic" but mixed strongly contrasting elements such as silk and leather, defining a romanticism that was also a bit camp, a bit punk. Gianni scored his first goal with this collection: a silk blouse bearing a wide, pleated collar seduced Diana Vreeland, former editor in chief of *Vogue* America and at that time consultant for the Costume Institute of the Metropolitan Museum of New York. She bought the blouse for herself. "Dear Gianni," Vreeland wrote him, "with your blouse on I felt like I was 20 years old again...." *Vogue* rated the piece the "top of the year" in its July lead story. This single item, blessed by the eccentric and highly influential Vreeland and by the bible of fashion, made Gianni a star in America. And that collection, playing on the contrast between leather pants and silk blouses, remains one of the favorites of Franca Sozzani, editor in chief of *Vogue Italia*.

The next season, Versace came out with an utterly different collection, dubbed Spaziale ("space-age") and inspired by the movies, that is, by George Lucas's *Star Wars*—but which also included references to classical antiquity in its draped tunics, and hints of sport in the reinforced shoulders, like those of American football players. Versace at his best borrowed lavishly from worlds that were light years away from one another and from diverse time frames, then remixed them all with his own personal, very arbitrary and bold syncretism. He said of those years: "In the 1970s I began to play with my restlessness, trying to find a way to put together diverse forms and materials as no one had ever done before. In those days, the first contrasts were born in my fashions, contrasts that would become the key to all my ideas. The mixings of past and present, of leather and silk, that came to me spontaneously reflected a desire to see two faces to everything: an elegant, traditional face, and an avant-garde face. The face of the past and the face of the future."

In the early 1970s, the young Versace made another acquaintance who would prove strategic to his career: Giovina Moretti, owner of the leading boutique showing multiple designers on Milan's Via della Spiga. She remembers their first encounter: "I had just opened the shoe shop Maud Frizon. A young man, rather shy, came in to ask if I could give him some boots and shoes for a small collection he was showing. It was customary to give out free samples to young designers who were beginning to make a name for themselves so I asked him who he was. 'My name is Gianni Versace, I come from Reggio Calabria, and I'm crazy about fashion,' he said. We started right off using the *tu* between us because there was an immediate sympathy. I gave him about thirty pairs of shoes. In turn, he offered to help me decorate my shop windows, as a way of paying me back. I told him that wasn't necessary, because I love to follow young people who are starting out in fashion. Some time later when he was working for Complice, Versace designed a collection that I've always thought of as "Rustic," with fabulous *jupons*, great flowered petticoats. I fell in love with what he was doing then. And out of that grew, for both of us, a new direction."

In 1977 Giò Moretti decided to open a shop named Versace. Her move was a little unorthodox, because Gianni did not yet have a collection with his own name on it. In the flourishing ready-to-wear market, Gianni was responsible for three lines—Genny, Callaghan and Complice. "When I told him what I wanted to do, Gianni objected that he didn't yet have his own line," Moretti recalls. "So I made him a proposal, that he and I would select items from the three lines right after the runway show, before the clothes went to the showrooms for the buyers. We'd take off the tags and sell the clothes as exclusives." Arnaldo Girombelli, producer of the collections, tried to buy some time when he heard of the proposal, but though he wasn't happy about it, he realized he had to accept this new arrangement. The first Gianni Versace shop was launched on March 28. The decor reflected the style of an artisan's workroom—*pietra grigia* stone floors, plain wooden benches—because that's how Gianni wanted it. Franca Versace came for the opening, looking proud as she surveyed the boutique with her son's name on it. Fashionable Milan was also there, curious about this new name, sipping cocktails from Saint Andrews (this restaurant on the corner of Via della Spiga and Via Sant'Andrea in the heart of the shopping district had just become the official caterer for Milano Collezioni, the fashion showcase at the Milan Fair). They admired the flesh and blood models in Versace's Spaziale collection by Callaghan. Contessa Francesca Vacca Agusta, who had previously worn only Valentino, now became Versace's great client.

"Gianni was a genius, and when it came to work he was totally positive," says Giovina Moretti. "In the ten years we worked closely together, I learned a great deal from him, and above all one thing—to keep on reading, informing myself, to be curious about everything. He was extraordinarily curious."

CHAPTER 3
Debut

Milan was now the coming place for the fashionable ready-to-wear business that was just taking off in Italy. The new names in stylish prêt-à-porter, having left behind the Sala Bianca of Palazzo Pitti where so many of them had showed for years, had migrated here. They were designing avant-garde clothes for industrial producers, at first in series so small they were called "between" because they were halfway between couturier and the mass market. They included, among the most innovative designers, Krizia, Caumont, Missoni, Enrico Coveri, Mila Schön, Laura Biagiotti, Sportmax of the Max Mara group of Reggio Emilia, Basile, Fendi, Giorgio Armani, Gianfranco Ferré. In just two years, between 1976 and 1978, the number of fashion houses on the official calendar of the National Chamber of Fashion grew from fourteen to fifty-two, and that was after a tough competition had winnowed down the hundreds of candidates. There were now also hundreds of journalists coming in from around the world, and thousands of buyers. They trekked to shows held both in individual locations chosen by the designers, and at the Milan Fair, where in 1978, Beppe Modenese (whom *Time* would soon be calling "Italy's fashion ambassador") created the Modit and Milano Collezioni fairs, the new showcases for Italian ready-to-wear.

"The reasons for Milan's prominence lie in the city itself, its Mitteleuropean position, its outlying territory full of textile producers, silk industries and shoemakers, its world-class concentration of design talent, its capacity for organization, its image, its prices," wrote the late Maria Pezzi, one of Italy's first and sharpest fashion journalists, in *Il Giorno*. "But it's also due to the fact that only in Milan has prêt-à-porter found its perfect physiognomy, its unique look, its cultural mark. Its *Italian style*."

Here, before an exclusive crowd of fashion-world experts, 32-year-old Gianni Versace debuted. Officially, the Versace label was first seen at the Museo della Permanente on March 28, 1978, a few days before the opening of the shop under his name, with a collection of womenswear for fall-winter 1978–1979. Versace had to prepare, as usual, his three lines, Genny, Callaghan and Complice and so he showed only a limited collection, which pursued some of the themes of Complice. The overall look that year was military style and Gianni had his own take on that: a very masculine coat, but with a highly feminine waist pulled in breathlessly tight by a belt, and feminine pleats sewn one over the other on the skirt. Leather was a key material in his show because Gianni wanted to explore the ways it could be worked and styled. That play between masculine-military and feminine-seductive was also seen in his evening wear, with safari jackets of georgette worn with sequined bandoleer belts.

There was a lot of leather in his following collection, spring-summer 1979, too, but the jackets were featherweight, hanging open in the front and pinned to the hips with wide suede sashes inspired by the obi of the Japanese kimono, a theme also visible in his Callaghan collection. Six months earlier, Versace had traveled to Japan. "I've taken everything I think is interesting and interpreted it in a European language, but very simply," Gianni told an interviewer. "The more I worked at it, the more I wondered why Japanese designers haven't yet emerged, with all the cultural wealth that country has." For Versace, so drawn to beauty and to cultural heritage, the absence of Japanese fashion made no sense. Only a few years later, in 1982, Japanese fashion designers did come to Europe, making a home for themselves in Paris. In his evening wear in that same collection, Gianni offered his so-called Starlet look inspired by the films of the fifties, in his own version, of course: cut down like lingerie in the lightest of fabrics layered one upon the other. It was a first taste of a style that would become one of his signatures, underclothes worn as outerwear.

His real debut with a full collection took place on March 27, 1979, and the 32-year-old Versace had a new companion at his side, American model Paul Beck. The collection for fall-winter 1979–1980 was shown at the Museo della Permanente on a set decorated with giant TV screens. The mood of the moment decreed that the ladylike look was in. It was time for the tailored suit and the redingote, an elegant coat with a tightly defined waist, for luxurious fabrics, for high heels. Versace stayed with the trend except for the heels, showing shoes with half-heels and even flats. His collection was dedicated to the flower. *Vogue Italia* picked as its lead item his clothes constructed like flower petals, both for day (flannel showing its lining of silk) and for evening, in feminine chiffon. Throughout the line, he used a lot of embroidery, such as the flower motifs etched on his sheepskin redingotes. Departing from what he had shown before, in this show Gianni envisioned a woman who was rather traditional, rather romantic. The change disoriented his buyers, who were used to a more aggressive, more pared-down look. Versace himself later said this collection was one that least represented him.

And the Italian fashion journalists were fairly cool. Natalia Aspesi, commenting in *la Repubblica* about the overall mood for that season, wrote, "The woman of the eighties is a woman who has finally gotten her act together and she wants us to remember that. Six months ago the designers shortened, tightened and split her skirts, they stuffed her into high heels, they rudely suggested she wiggle her hips and show herself off. And all that furious exhibitionism has now paid off. They've found her a prosperous husband and they want to make her, at all costs, into that dreadful, chilling thing, 'a real lady,' a lady loaded with those dusty virtues that disguise all her feminine frailty and inexplicably reassure men and fill them with pride: class, charm, style, chic, allure, even distinction." Another fashion commentator, Adriana Mulassano of the *Corriere della Sera*, wrote of Versace: "Let's look at one of our leading prêt-à-porter designers,

Gianni Versace, who in eight years of work has won us all over precisely with his extraordinary sense of modernity, because he has always designed for a woman of his time. This season, though, Versace has done a complete about-face, focusing far too much on sheer runway impact, offering clothes for a rarefied, sophisticated public, gags like tweed jackets over full taffetta skirts, black nappa leather jackets over lace and georgette dresses. We're rooting for the Other Versace, who in the same collection offered gorgeous three-quarter-length sheepskin coats embroidered on the wool side; gray raincoats with a marvelous new umbrella-style cut and brightly-colored satin linings."

Hebe Dorsey, the venerable fashion editor of the *International Herald Tribune*, agreed. "Young Gianni Versace launched his first 'solitary' collection and there were problems: the philosophy was confused, the clothes lacked fresh ideas and looked like they'd already been seen. What happened to that talent that so impressed us in the last few years? The collections created for Callaghan, Genny and Complice were in fact rich and exciting. But maybe that's just the problem: Versace continues to work for those three labels. And designing four collections a season is just too much. For anyone."

Certainly it was a heavy commitment. But by doing so many collections, "Gianni Versace breathed different atmospheres, he sensed the mood," says Beppe Modenese. "And overwork also suited him. Gianni, the outsider with such great talent, had such a desire to work and he transmitted that enthusiam, that curiosity, to all those who worked with him and to friends. And he was beloved for that generosity of spirit."

The Other Versace that Adriana Mulassano spoke of was in fact the real Versace, who quickly rediscovered himself and his strong, unmistakable look. For the following season, spring-summer 1980, he launched the Optical style. He matched his finely striped black and white blouses with white piquet, "ladylike" materials fashioned, however, without any buttons, showing bare skin beneath. Striped dresses opened to the belt at the waist, red leotards underneath. *Vogue Italia* wrote that the new Versace look "even in its geometrical cut and graphic ornamentation, shows an affinity with tunics and peplums and therefore represents a step forward compared to hardline severity." The comment went on: "The fact that he hasn't broken the thread that ties him to the neoclassical period and to ancient Greece, that he's been able to accommodate new ideas without abandoning the crux of his style, is this designer's great strength."

Hebe Dorsey, writing for the *Herald Tribune*, reversed her severe judgment on the previous season with a kind of hymn to this one: "This time at Gianni Versace, we found a designer who is much more courageous and enterprising, more creative and able to impress fashion veterans. In fact it is he who brings us the novelty of the season, the Optical style that so effortlessly invaded his runway and which is young, fresh, new and seductive. We'll be hearing about him for some time."

The moment had come for Versace to dedicate his efforts to his own label. He left Complice, the line he was most strongly identified with, to concentrate on the Gianni Versace brand. One of its strengths lay in the gorgeous knitwear produced by Mario Bandiera's Les Copains, Gianni's first partner for the Istante collection (it had been withdrawn from the market in 1979). For the fall-winter 1980–1981 collection, Gianni presented an idea he had originally devised for menswear—jackets and trousers based on riding gear—and the style was incredibly successful in the shops because it offered a classy, original approach to sportswear. Italy's leading socialites were quickly captured by the new look. One of them was Wanda Galtrucco, queen of Milan drawing rooms and even those beyond Milan, who introduced Versace to all the right people. "I began to wear Versace from that collection onward; I owned all the different versions of those little jackets paired to those fabulous silky nappa trousers. I already knew Gianni from the days when he visited Milan with his mother to make purchases for the shop in Reggio Calabria. And I was buying Callaghan, Genny and Complice. Until 1980 I wore Valentino haute couture, then I began to wear Versace."

Even Mariuccia Mandelli, the woman behind Krizia, bought a pair of those Versace trousers. Astonishing, because in a world of prima donnas like that of fashion, designers rarely if ever let it be known they appreciate a rival's work. Versace had now fallen in love with trousers. "Why trousers? Because they are more modern, more eighties," he said. "I like to see them everywhere, even under a skirt...." And they turned every which way in the spring- summer 1981 collection, one that would be a great commercial success: pants that were open and fluttering, or tightly cut and cropped at the calf under a wrapped skirt, in a grand mix of extravagant geometric patterns and boisterous florals.

Versace was in a hurry. Just a few months after his first womenswear collection, he launched his menswear line in September. It was right on target. Versace's man wore urban sportswear, blazers of bouclé wool and suede trousers with three waist pleats, wide at the hips and narrow at the hem. The American men's fashion magazine *Gentlemen's Quarterly*, reporting in August 1979, wrote enthusiastically of Versace, calling him a "well-known European designer." The Americans liked this "tidy-but-disheveled" masculine fashion. But Versace kept going forward. He left sportswear behind and moved into formal elegance. For the spring-summer 1980 collection, next to pullovers inspired by American football, he showed well-constructed jackets that harked back to classic masculine tailoring, but with details that floored everyone, such as the pastels he showed them in—rose, sky blue, yellow. He spelled out his philosophy: "If you want to imagine the ideal man to wear this kind of Italian fashion, think of a young American who has studied in Europe, in France or Italy—a cross between the American physique and a Latin mentality and taste." Donatella was now constantly by his side. She was backstage at all his shows, learning everything there was to learn.

His mother, however, was no longer with him; she died in 1978. The relationship with his father continued to be difficult for Gianni. Papà Antonio didn't come to see the clothes his son sent out on the runways in glitzy Milan. He didn't participate, except very distractedly and from far away, in Gianni's international success. He remained down in Reggio Calabria, in the world of Gianni's past. In the summer, the few times he could, Gianni joined his brother and sister in the family house in front of the sea. There, in August 1979, something happened that Gianni always remembered with strong feeling. He talked about it to Claudio Altarocca in an interview in *La Stampa* in the 1990s. "It was a terrible summer of muggy heat and cinders, the cinders that the wind sometimes carries over from Sicily." It was morning, and Gianni was waiting in the empty house for his father to appear. He could hear, from the other rooms, feminine voices in his mother's atelier. Lunchtime came, but his father still had not appeared. His absence was peculiar. Gianni began calling his friends, his relatives, but no one had any idea where Antonio might be, and no one had seen him. Three o'clock in the afternoon came; then it was four. At a certain point, Gianni suddenly understood. He said to his brother Santo, "Do you know where we'll find him? At the cemetery."

They hurried up there, high on the hills over Reggio. "It's beautiful, our cemetery," said Gianni. "There's always a breath of wind and the scent of orange blossom floats through the trees." The family chapel is made of local *pietra grigia* stone. Gianni and Santo raced over. Inside they found their father sitting on a stool between two empty tombs, in front of Franca's, which was decorated with myrtle. "He seemed to be lost, abandoned; he had aged a hundred years." And there in the chapel, something significant happened for Gianni. "We embraced each other. I had found my father again. I felt him close to me for the first time." For young Versace, it was as if he had surpassed the years of childhood and adolescence, when his interests and his life hadn't met his father's expectations. "We embraced without speaking. And we all cried. Our whole life came back to me, my mother, the South with all its bright sunshine and all its sadness. My father got up; we went home. It was a very tender afternoon. I managed to get him to laugh a little. We were in the kitchen, sitting around the white marble table, and we all had a *granita di caffè*, and then we had a lemon *granita*. We moved into the sitting room and we were all silent again. There was no sound at all coming from outside, yet I could feel that my past was outside, all those years that I went to the sea and to Aspromonte, the vacations that were the same every year, the trips to the lake and the woods, the evenings with the Americans from the NATO base at Montalto. My father would come to spend the weekends with us in Aspromonte. If I am the person I am today, it is because I had this happy, healthy childhood, so full of love."

From that moment on, matters between Gianni and his father became more serene. They often spoke on the phone. Every year at Christmas they would get together at Gianni's villa at Moltrasio on Lake Como. Gianni bought this first house in 1980 thinking right from the start that it would be the place where he united the family around him, a ritual that was reassuring and necessary for him.

But Gianni took few vacations. He worked and worked. From the beginning a young accountant, Claudio Luti, assisted him; Claudio was smart and ambitious and helped Gianni negotiate his first contracts. Gianni's brother Santo had introduced him to Claudio, whom Santo had met while doing his military service. The two were first at officers' training school in Caserta, and then were sub-lieutenants in the Genova Cavalleria regiment at Palmanova near Udine in northeast Italy. Santo and Claudio ate together, took their leaves together, became friends. Claudio, like Santo, had a degree in business economics and had opened an office in Milan. With Gianni he got to know the ready-to-wear business just at the magic moment when it was taking off in Italy. He knew Ferrante, Tositti and Monti's company FTM, which sold designer clothes not through salesmen who went to visit clients, but by getting the most important clients to visit their collections in Milan. "Fashion interested me right away," says Luti. "And I began to work as an accountant for others in the business." Gianni was already designing for Callaghan and Genny and would soon be handling Complice. He was a talented and prolific artist, but he also had an eye for business. And he felt he was ready to strike out on his own.

"And so," continues Luti, "in 1977 in Milan we founded Gianni Versace S.r.l. with 20 million lire capital. In the meantime, Gianni opened his office on Via della Spiga. And he and Santo asked me if I would devote myself exclusively to the new company. For a while, I went back and forth between my office and Versace. And then I joined this new venture, which I found so attractive. We created a new Gianni Versace company, whose partners were Gianni, Santo and myself with a minority share. It owned the Gianni Versace brand and controlled its advertising. We also founded GiviModa, which had exclusive rights to sell clothes from the Versace collections. So our group, from the beginning, controlled design, distribution and communication. We sent the orders to Greppi and Girombelli, who in turn produced the clothes, shipped them to the clients and collected payment. Greppi and Girombelli paid us for the services we provided, supplying us percentages that meant we had secure earnings, with no risk." There was no risk, assuming, that is, that all went according to plan: that the collections were admired (and Gianni's were ever-more admired), and the budget forecasts accurate, so that the manufacturers produced the right number of each model, neither too many nor too few.

"With this business structure, we were doubling our sales from one collection to another, without ever growing too big too fast." Luti was named chief executive officer alongside Santo, who was also CEO of the group as well as chairman. Following the same model, they drew up contracts with other manufacturers—Mario Bandera of Les Copains for knitwear, Giacomo Corsi for leather, Sergio

Rossi for shoes—to fill out Gianni's collections. "This three-way control," Luti recalls, "allowed us to open Gianni Versace boutiques, beginning in the United States, at the best addresses and with the partners we wanted. Singapore, Miami, New York: everywhere these shops were the best of all possible publicity for Versace. We were among the first to employ franchising, making arrangements with the retailers and insisting that the spaces be designed by architects Rocco Magnoli and Lorenzo Carmellini, who worked under Gianni's orders. In those days, franchising existed only in the U.S. I remember that the first contract of this kind we signed was called an 'insignia contract' because there was no name for it in Italian law."

In these same years the Versace manufacturing hub was born, in partnership with Greppi from Callaghan and Gigi Monti. Alias, as it was called, "began as a single room inside Greppi's Zamasport facility," explains Luti. "Then we bought out Greppi and Monti's shares to take 100 percent. And Alias grew little by little to become a huge manufacturing firm in Novara, where the better part of the Versace collection is produced. In the mid-1980s, Versace S.r.l. became a shareholding company, and we created a holding. I remained a partner of all the companies and CEO of the group until 1987. Then I decided to move on. I sold the Versace brothers my shares and with the returns, two months later I bought Kartell,[1] and I'm still chairman there. From my point of view, the time had come. But my

---

1. A leading company in the plastics business.

experience with Versace was fascinating. There was such a charge of enthusiasm in that company, among retailers and distributors, such a strong company loyalty. I remember Gianni's runway shows, him re-pinning up the hems the night before, making changes all over the place. And then all of us in the room hearing the clothes swishing, seeing eyes sparkling, people applauding. I learned so much from Gianni. He would read mountains of magazines, all incredibly quickly. I remember one time in New York, we had just gotten off the plane, and he bought an armful at the newstand—and not just fashion magazines—and by the time I met up with him at the car he had already flipped through them and and marked what interested him. He wanted to learn from every field—theater, music, ballet, films—and he did so with great humility. I'm sure that at a certain point he would have been fully capable of staging a stage performance himself. He wanted to grow. And he was growing every day as a person, as a designer, as a lover of the arts. He had inexhaustible energy. And not just that. If we were going to visit a firm, we had to get there before the workers arrived, and then, okay, when the meeting was over we could sleep in the car on the way back. Those are two things above all that I learned from Gianni: respect for hard work, and not to be satisfied, ever."

When the company was created, Gianni already had a logo in mind. It would be the Medusa, one of the three Gorgon daughters of Phorcys and Ceto, winged monsters with a thicket of snakes in place of hair. Versace chose this image in honor of the Magna Graecia of his origins, and with a childhood memory in mind: the remains of an ancient Roman mosaic in Reggio Calabria near which he used to play soccer. Later he would say: "When I had to choose a symbol, I thought of that ancient myth: those who fall in love with the Medusa have no way back. So why not imagine that those whom Versace conquers—that they, too, cannot go back?"

CHAPTER 4
Avedon, Please!

What photographer could create the right image for his fashion? Gianni Versace began thinking about this question immediately after his first big show. It was the spring of 1979, and as always, he wanted the best. At first he thought of the elegant, glossy Irving Penn, who had been launched in the 1940s by the editor in chief of *Vogue* America at that time, Alexander Liberman. Penn is something of a living legend for his formal sophistication, the simplicity of his compositions, his eclectic range. Versace met him in New York and told him he would be delighted if Penn would do his advertising campaign. Penn, a reserved, even shy, man, drew back: "Look," he said, "I'm not much good at fashion, I only know how to do flowers.[1] But there's a young fellow who's very good at fashion: his name is Richard Avedon." Avedon wasn't in truth much younger than Penn; he was 56 years old. And he was already legendary. Twenty years before, Truman Capote had written a stunning profile of Avedon for his most famous book of photographs, *Observations*. Avedon,

---

1. Penn was then working on his series "Flowers," photographs of beautiful, wilting flowers.

wrote Capote, had been a precocious child who pinned up Steichen and Man Ray photos on his bedroom walls. He had studied photography during his military service, and then, while taking classes at the New School for Social Research, he met Alexey Brodovitch, the influential art director at *Harper's Bazaar*, who taught a class in experimental photography.

At the end of the war, Brodovitch gave Avedon his start. He began to work regularly for *Harper's Bazaar* and *Life*, and soon he was appearing in a vast number of photography shows. A hard worker and tireless perfectionist, Avedon was known for making up to sixty prints of a single negative to get just the density of light he wanted. In the 1960s he was America's most successful and highest-paid photographer. He would also be the most influential from a formal point of view, and even today a great many photographers take him as their model.

Avedon was very eclectic, but he liked doing portraits above all. He shot celebrities from every field, from Pablo Picasso to Marilyn Monroe, from Charlie Chaplin to Coco Chanel, from the Duke and Duchess of Windsor to Jean Cocteau, from Marella Agnelli to Janis Joplin and Maria Callas. Not to mention the most famous fashion models of the day: the slender Dovima in an elegant Dior gown among the elephants of the circus; Elise Daniels and Monique wearing marvelous Schiaparelli hats and smoking cigarettes at Paris's famous Café de Flore; a stupendous Suzy Parker in Lanvin on the stage of the Folies Bergère. Avedon also liked photographing working people, and captured, in his matchless black-and-white images, miners, chambermaids, ranch hands, hospital patients and New Mexico secretaries. All in all, he was a living treasure. Young Versace contacted him through Paul Beck and met him in his white-walled New York studio decorated all in white.

Until then, Gianni had used high-quality Italian photographers, but no better than that. Now, with a strong firm behind him, the time for a quantum leap had come. True to his nature, he took a path that was in some ways against the grain. To photograph his so very determinedly modern clothes, he wanted someone who was the epitome of formal perfection, the cutting edge of fifties photography, a man who in many ways was already a classic. Avedon's first advertising campaign for Versace showed beachwear for spring-summer 1980, and the press declared it a success. There were several models in the shot, a woman and two men; in one picture, one man is holding the woman in his arms and she is running her hands through his hair, while the other is crouched at her feet, his arms wrapped around one of her legs. In another photo the woman, wearing a one-piece suit that plunges both front and back, seems about to pull off one man's trousers, while the second lies flat on the floor, eyes shut. This was Gianni's style seen through Avedon's lens: several figures on the set, a powerfully sexy atmosphere, but also a decidedly ironic one.

When the fall-winter 1980–1981 collection appeared, Avedon's photographs showed the first groups of male and female models, all standing up. In 1981, the famous photos of models clustered around a dressmaker appeared, and then groups of figures lying one next to the other, almost like group sex scenes against elegant, all-but-chaste satin backdrops. In *The Naked and the Dressed: 20 Years of Versace by Avedon* (with its cover photo of Elton John made up like a woman and wearing a Versace chain mail dress), we find all the names of the models, just the way the subjects of portraits are always identified. There are Jerry Hall, Rosie Vela, Jason Savas, Alessandro, Beverly Johnson, Kelly LeBrock, Rene Russo, Iman, Brooke Shields. The theatrical way Avedon typically photographed people lent Versace's fashion a unique look—whether it be a dress of slippery metal mesh, a stretch of bold black skin, or a sensual spill of velvet drapery. "The partnership between Avedon and Versace was one of the most successful in the entire history of fashion," says Giovanni Gastel, a fashion photographer who worked often for Versace. "The look Avedon created for Versace is unforgettable, and remains even today the Versace point of reference for all of us in the business. Avedon created a language, the Avedon language for Versace. First of all, he invented a type of woman, the Versace woman, who was a mixture of explosiveness, sensuality and elegance. And then he invented a sort of international high society that didn't really exist, but which seemed true to life. And he broadened the value of the label, imagining that something like that—a luxurious, sensual way of life with the characteristics he pictured—would effectively come to exist."

Avedon shot Versace's first advertising campaigns in New York. Then Gianni asked him to come to Milan and the great photographer decided he didn't mind leaving his golden cocoon. He was getting record fees, naturally— even larger than those he was paid in the fat American market. "I have an emotional memory of the meeting between the artist Avedon and the artist Versace," says Alfredo Albertone, a keen expert on Avedon and photo editor of the Italian fashion magazines *D* and *Velvet*. "In the 1980s, I was 19 years old and a studio assistant at *Donna*, a magazine that was then assembling an extraordinary school of Italian photographers, from Oliviero Toscani, to Fabrizio Ferri, to Giovanni Gastel. It was an effervescent moment, and to see Avedon's formal mastery and his expressive power applied to clothes that were as gorgeous and modern as Versace's was like getting a whiff of pure oxygen. With all due modesty, it seems to me that the artistic marriage between Versace and Avedon represented one of the high points in the advertising of Italian luxury goods worldwide."

In 1980, Donatella Versace became the stylist for Gianni's advertising campaigns. More and more often, she was working with Paul Beck, the handsome, cultivated former model who was Gianni's partner. They spent their intense workdays together and often went out together in the evening. Gianni was never a late-night guy, nor was he much interested in social life; he got up early in the morning and hardly ever stopped working. So in a sense, it was almost predestined that Donatella would fall for Paul. And Paul for her. Gianni didn't miss anything, and this fact didn't elude him either. For a while, he pretended not to notice. Then the evidence became too strong to ignore. He had a terrible fight with Donatella and Paul left, not to return until he had made up his mind. Paul chose the diminutive Donatella, every bit as tough as her brother and quite a bit younger. He and Donatella married in 1983, fulfilling his dream of having a family, the dream of every good American. They wed in the church of Moltrasio, the town on Lake Como where Gianni had his villa. And so all would be healed in the bosom of the family. For Gianni, it was a hard blow, a tough time. Only work and his insatiable curiosity, his hunger for new cultural inspiration, his drive to go forward and discover the world as it was changing, enabled him to endure that harsh moment.

Professional success compensated for personal disappointment. His fortunate partnership with Avedon continued, with a few interruptions, for some twenty years. It was a special relationship, as both Avedon and Versace would testify. Avedon, talking to Chiara Beria di Argentine for *L'Espresso* in 1993, explained that after a period dedicated to portraits he was then returning to fashion photography, but only for Versace. "At the moment, I'm not interested in photographing beautiful women. I'm not dealing with women now; I'm dealing with apocalyptic issues." Versace was the only exception. Why? "Because he's a man who is generous both in spirit and in soul. Versace never comes to tell me how I should work. He just says, 'Here are the clothes, do your magic and I'll pay you.' I can't think of any other client who behaves that way. I don't even really understand it, but I know that he has a big heart, and great love and respect for art and artists. It's rare; he's special. If you photograph for Revlon or Chanel or Ralph Lauren, it's work. These are huge firms with giant balance sheets. You spell out your idea for them, they hold a meeting, approve it and so forth. With Versace, it's different. When I come to Italy, I am his guest. When I work in New York, his sister Donatella and brother-in-law Paul are there. The first thing we do is set up lunch in the studio. A plate of pasta, very simple, as always."

It was because of Versace's friendship with the American photographer that the so-called "supermodels" first appeared on Milan's runways. Versace persuaded these big names to leave Paris, where they had been working exclusively, and come to Italy. He wanted them to wear his sexy, outrageous clothes, to glide down his runway, to sparkle on the pages of his advertisements. He offered them astronomical sums. And they came to Milan, where each of these goddesses could earn a fortune with a week of fashion shows.

Stephanie Seymour arrived first. Avedon photographed her for Versace for the first time in 1988. About her, he said: "Stephanie Seymour is an exception. She has something others don't have; she has humanity. Once I shot her while she was lifting her skirt, and underneath she was naked. It was a strange image. She's not puritanical, but neither is she seductive. She's not offering anything, just affirming herself. That's why Stephanie interests me." Take a look at the photo of her on all fours over Marcus and you can't but agree. He's naked, she's got on a military overcoat and black leather boots with studs and her hair is flying. "The others," said Avedon, "from Christy Turlington to Linda Evangelista, are certainly all splendid, but they are cold; perfect, but empty. Look at the expressions on their faces: they are far-away expressions. The gods and goddesses are always detached, for when one is beautiful everything comes too easily and one is shielded from normal human feelings," said the ever-so-sophisticated Avedon. But for that generation, all of those models—from Cindy Crawford to Claudia Schiffer, from Elle MacPherson, familiarly known as The Body, to the more maternal Helena Christensen, to the aggressive Naomi Campbell—stood for the glamour that the stars of Hollywood had represented in the fifties and sixties. Famous, as highly paid as rock stars, for a very long time they embodied the feminine ideal in the global village; they were as well known in Hong Kong as in Europe and the U.S. They took it all from the great fashion circus of the decade: all the most prestigious runways, all the lipstick, perfume and makeup ads for the most glorious, glamorous brands. But among the insiders, they would always be thought of as *Versace's* supermodels.

Stephanie and her fellow fashion models even staked out a place in the museum world. In 1995, with Versace as his sponsor, Richard Avedon mounted his most beautiful exhibit ever, in the Sala delle Cariatidi of Milan's Palazzo Reale. Called *Evidence 1944–1994*, it traced Avedon's entire life's work and included wonderful blowups of his fashion work, his portraits and his street scenes. There was also a sequence of photos taken of his father when the older man was ill, right up until eight days before he died. "They show a face that appears ever more immobile, ever more carved-out," wrote Italian critic Arturo Carlo Quintavalle, "where life is slowly drawing back from the taut skin to concentrate in the intense, almost glassy gaze. They speak of a tender, yet very determined, almost bitter, dialogue between Avedon and his own roots." For Avedon, Quintavalle went on, "to make a portrait is to hold a dialogue with another person; it doesn't matter whom you shoot, for life is full of protagonists, whether they be jobless persons from the Midwest, or the executive on Wall Street." Gianni Versace, who had chosen Avedon to render his clothes immortal, certainly adored Avedon for just this omnivorous approach to life. It was, after all, so very much like his own.

CHAPTER 5
Rivals

In 1980 Versace and Giovina Moretti set up their second Gianni Versace boutique, on Via Bocca di Leone in Rome. Opening night was the social event of the season: everyone who counted as a celebrity in Rome was there, the blue bloods, the show business world, and all the glossy fashionistas. Giò Moretti has a particular memory of that evening: "There were Gianni and Donatella, who were holding hands, looking each other in the eyes. And she said to him, 'Just think if Mamma were here, how happy she'd be.' " Gianni was happy that night, too. He needed success, he needed to see that people liked his clothes, he needed to feel loved. The recent critical comments of certain Italian journalists hadn't slid off his back easily. No, the young designer up from Calabria loaded with talent and energy and keen to show it had suffered from those criticisms. He asked himself: "Why shouldn't I be loved in Milan? I work hard, I try to make women more beautiful and feminine, and yet the critics aren't that enthusiastic." The fact was, Milan was also Giorgio Armani's town.

When Versace showed his first collection in 1979, Armani had already been on the scene since 1975. Armani was twelve years older than Versace; he had followed the scientific high school curriculum in the Lombardy city of Piacenza and had once dreamed of being a doctor. When I interviewed him some years back, he described himself this way: "I've never been a tailor. I never made clothes for dolls. I began to learn something about fashion when I worked for the Rinascente department store as a consultant with the buyers, to help even out the flow of orders coming in. The job suited my esthetic sense, but I didn't have the sacred fire of fashion in me. The next step was a job with a company called Hitman that did menswear. It was a good firm but somewhat stale; it needed a *designer*, a term that in those days, in the second half of the 1960s, still had a somewhat vague significance. In 1973 I opened a studio of my own with Sergio Galeotti. There were three of us: Sergio, myself and the secretary in the studio on Corso Venezia. I realized that our professional profile was taking off when one day, while I was drawing and Sergio was next door selling my clothes to Bergdorf Goodman, I heard that Bergdorf's wanted to devote a corner to Armani."

In 1978, Armani and Galeotti got their big opportunity. The Gruppo Finanziario Tessile (GFT) owned by Marco Rivetti, one of Italy's leading clothing manufacturers, desperately wanted higher quality in its ready-to-wear fashions. In Milan, Armani's name was mentioned. After long negotiations, Armani and Galeotti signed a deal with GFT that would never be matched in fashion history. GFT would produce the Giorgio Armani prêt-à-porter label, while the label remained the property of Giorgio Armani S.p.A. Armani could keep on working for other firms as a consultant while Giorgio Armani S.p.A. designed the clothes that Rivetti was licensed to produce.

Armani's 1970s collections all revolved around a precise notion that took the jacket as its starting point. "The first jackets were intended for women who had come out of the women's movement," said Armani. "They were women who worked, completely the opposite of the flower child look that was so popular then. I discovered this uniform: a man's jacket, very simple, without lady's darts and tucks, destructured, with pockets—something you could move freely in, in keeping with the new requirements of contemporary life. My style was called classic, but in fact it was something more complicated, because it was sophisticated, anything but the typical lady's suit of the 1940s. And behind it, there was a concept of 'democracy' there, because these were clothes designed for a dynamic existence, for women who moved around in small cars, not in carriages or limousines."

Nothing could be further from the clothes designed by Gianni Versace: his wild and crazy shapes, those madly-mixed metaphors, that hot femininity. *Repubblica*'s reporter Silvia Giacomoni drew out the contrast between the two designers in a book written in the early 1980s. "Versace comes from Calabria, he's a product of the South who insists on surrounding himself, even in Milan, with the affection and help of his whole family. The offspring of a dressmaker who owned a boutique, Versace declares himself a 'tailor's son.' With that particular melancholy of the immigrant made good, he transforms the Magna Graecia of his youth into a land of heroes. The plumed helmet, the broken column—these are his limits, but he doesn't know that, and he pursues his destiny as an artist who wants to be recognized as such in the world of art."

Meanwhile, wrote Giacomoni, "Giorgio Armani doesn't want to design clothes that 'enhance,' as Versace does. His clothes have so far been an effort to reinvent fashion, so that those who want to be elegant aren't condemned to be out-moded. Armani does his best to demolish the myth of the artist and present himself as an ordinary, if excellent, professional who works in the clothing industry. He just doesn't succeed at convincing us of that." Neither he, nor any other designer in those years when the ready-to-wear business was taking off. Because, continued Giacomoni, "the aura that the French couturiers, who dressed the thirty richest and most beautiful women in the world, had created around themselves, quickly migrated to the Italian designer, who had the cleverness to know how to design for 30,000. Faced with him, all irony, all critical faculties, are silenced. Admiration is de rigueur."

In these years, fashion began to emanate a new dimension, becoming more and more a reflection of cultural directions, symbolic statements, styles of life. The designer, whether he liked it or not, had become a charismatic figure. Armani tried to defend himself with his willed understatement. For Versace the problem didn't exist; he was—he felt himself to be—an artist. It was obvious that the contest would be, right from the beginning, between these two. They were the best, the strongest, the most courageous. They represented two types of women, or rather, two faces that usually coexist in a single woman—the classy lady and the seductress. Fashion journalists saw the rivalry right off: it wasn't a mystery. The comment that summed it up was made by Anna Wintour, then an editor at *Vogue* America, later to be the much-feared editor in chief. The Versace woman, she said, was always the mistress while the Armani woman was the wife. The two roles could, in theory, have coexisted. But in fact, it never happened that one designer's client also bought the clothes of the other. Armani, with his all-white minimalist runways, and Versace, with his performances on glistening blocks of black marble, were two, far apart, separate universes. Those who belonged to one camp never set foot in the other. It would be tasteless to do so. And tactless to treat the two designers that way.

Each of them had a well-placed lady by his side to organize his social life, to decide who among the establishment merited an invitation, and who in the arts and performance world should be called. Giorgio Armani relied on the impeccable savoir-faire (a savoir-faire that sometimes approached genuine brutality) of Giovanna Borletti, linked to Giorgio since the days in which the young designer got his start at Rinascente, then owned by the Borletti family. Her dinners, served up with sobriety and formal perfection on chaste white table settings, united Milan's best bourgeoisie: celebrities like the writer

Alain Elkann, once married to an Agnelli heiress, and top furniture designers like architect Ettore Sottsass, to name just two. Gianni Versace depended on Wanda Galtrucco, his longtime friend, to manage his social connections. She did this happily, opening the doors of Milan for him, and later those of London and New York.

"At first Gianni was not so well liked in Milan," she recalls. "My friends thought his clothes were too bold, too brassy. But then they all fell deeply in love with Gianni, all of them, from Enrica Invernizzi to Evelina Shapira, from the Orsi Mangelli sisters to Barbara Berlingeri—even my mother Eleonora Piccitto, who was then wearing only Valentino haute couture. Because the more you got to know Gianni, the more you liked his clothes. I was something like his companion; I was always there, even when he was at home. We liked the same things, we liked going to art exhibits, to antique dealers, to the cinema, the theater. The two of us with just a few other close friends, among them Gigi Scagliotti, who introduced me to Gianni in the early 1970s."

The two designers, Armani and Versace, could not have been two more different personalities. Journalist Andrea Lee, in a long interview with Versace published in *The New Yorker*, suggested to him that from a professional point of view, the competition between the two had been productive for Versace. He replied, "Yes, it was a stroke of luck for both of us to be constantly faced with our opposites. I dress a woman who is more beautiful, more seductive. I adore women. He, instead, dresses a type of woman who is sadder, a bit washed-out.

They call it *chic*. Personally, I've never seen anything chic in it, but we all have our own way of looking at things!" It's not easy to find as straightforward a comment on the matter from Armani, who has always liked to rely more on the art of innuendo.

"Giorgio Armani and Gianni Versace were perfect complements," says Gisella Borioli, editor in chief of *Donna* from 1980 to 1993. "During fashion week one of them would open the shows and the other one would close them, and you wouldn't have an idea of what the season's trend was until you had seen both. Versace was an extremist of the cutting edge, of display, of experimentation; he was a triumph of shapes and colors. Armani was an extremist of no-color, of sleekness, of consistency. Versace was inconsistent in his stylistic gyrations, he took a different route every time, he was an innovator. For instance, there was the time he showed leather jackets that instead of being stitched together, were sealed by thermofusion—and that's just one of the many examples one could cite. Armani built up his oeuvre without ever betraying his style. They were opposites in character, too, with two very different ways of relating to others."

"Once," Gisella Borioli adds, "a daily paper asked me to interview some designers, among them Armani and Versace. They laid out the story with pictures and quotes from the two 'rivals' next to each other. The comments the two had made were polite; there was no conflict there. But from Versace I got flowers with a note of thanks, while from Armani came an annoyed letter, because he hadn't liked that face-off between them. Armani was somewhat solitary, somewhat guarded; he defended his autonomy and his image. Versace was more easy-going, less concerned about the constant comparison. But then everything about the two designers was different. Versace's shows were spectacular, surprising, he had famous models on his runway, while Armani's shows were measured, with a few little coups de théâtre at the end, and anonymous models whose only job it was to show off the clothes. And then there were their second homes: in Miami for Versace; on the isle of Pantelleria and in Broni, near Pavia, for Armani. And the stars who lent their luster to the labels: for Versace, there was Madonna, while for Armani, there was Sophia Loren. They were two greats, like Bartali and Coppi[1] or the Milanese soccer clubs, Inter and Milan. They were the salt and pepper you needed to give some zip to fashion."

---

1. Gino Bartali and Fausto Coppi were famous rivals in Giro d'Italia bike racing of the 1940s and '50s.

CHAPTER 6

The Villa

Versace never stopped working. His days began early in the morning and continued, with just a break for lunch, into the evening. He was not the sort of designer to shut himself up in his atelier making sketches and drawings. His sketches were quick and simple, because he conceptualized an item of clothing in his mind, and he then proceeded by choosing a fabric, draping it on a tailor's dummy, looking at various print options, at colors and embroidery. Of course, the design process all began long before this, because Versace always observed everything around him, whether it was art books, fashion drawings, or catalogues of antiques. He went to see every art exhibit he could and sent for the catalogues of those he couldn't attend but which interested him. Someone recalled him gathering everything he could find about a faraway show of aborigine art in Sydney, Australia. And then he got out, he travelled. He studied people on the street, he went to the movies, to the theater. His brain seemed to be constantly processing things, faces, events, images, and these, stirred together and constantly renewed, became his great reservoir of inspiration. And then there was the commercial side, the business. Gianni decided everything, he always had the last word in meetings, after he had heard the opinions of all and carefully considered those of just a few. With three collections to send out twice a year, with a keen sense of responsibility for the many people who worked so hard to produce his sumptuous, complicated clothes, he needed a place of his own, somewhere to slow down and recharge.

He found this place in 1977, when he bought a tumbledown villa in Moltrasio, on the southwest branch of Lake Como, near Villa d'Este and other patrician and haut bourgeois residences like Villa Erba belonging to the Visconti di Modrone family, and the Volpi family's Villa Pizzo. The lakeside landscape is enchanting here: there are great gardens with mature beeches, plane trees, palms, yews and cedars that run right down to the lake, and behind them soft green hills, surrounded by Alpine peaks. The lake's waters are blue, turning pale gray when the mist descends. Versace fell in love with Villa Fontanelle; he liked everything about it including its impressive pedigree. Built on the shore of the lake in the first half of the 19th century by an eccentric Englishman, Lord Charles Curry, the property had changed hands a couple of times, going first to Antonio Besana, music lover and friend of Giuseppe Verdi, and then, after it passed to several members of his family, being sold to the Cambiaghi family. Versace bought it piece by piece, because the estate had already been broken up in parcels to be developed into many apartments with lakeside views. It cost him 1.5 billion lire, and he lovingly supervised the long rehab and restoration, which was carried out with scrupulous respect for the original layout of the house—a rectangular plan, three floors with a large central terrace. It took three years to rebuild it perfectly in the original neoclassical style.

To restore his garden, Versace called on Roy Strong, director of the Victoria and Albert Museum and a noted landscape designer. Strong came down to the villa and stayed there few days, taking some notes. "On my next visit," he recalls in his book *Do Not Disturb,* "Versace said to me, 'This, Roy, is your garden.' Of course it wasn't really true, because it was Versace's garden, transformed by the work of his imagination. Over the following years I watched that garden change and take shape. White lilies began to grow from a sparkling fountain that now has a pristine parterre in front. The lilies have multiplied in beds planted to either side. Medusa heads—framed by an arch covered with climbing vines—serve as wall fountains that spin out jets of water, while between them, Neptune brandishes his trident against a curtain of water. Statues have been planted everywhere and the flank of the hill now hosts a little army of gods and goddesses. Bright rows of purple pansies and beds of pink begonias testify to Versace's shameless delight in the precise use of gaudy colors." Sir Roy and his wife Lady Julia, a stage designer and also a garden lover, would be regular guests of Gianni at the villa each year in May when the roses bloomed. As soon as they could, Strong and Gianni went around Europe looking for new statues in stone and terra cotta.

Inside the house, Gianni indulged in his passion for all that was beautiful, with the help of Sergio Baroni, an antiques consultant and a dear friend who had been a humanities professor and once had a job at Versace's press office. "When it came to decorating," says Baroni, "Gianni had an extraordinary ability to size up an object immediately, even though he had no particular training. He could buy a painting, a chair, or a piece of furniture after giving it just a glance, or from a photo in a catalogue. He didn't care whether a drawer, a tabletop or a piece of the decor wasn't an authentic part of the original. What he was looking for was the overall decorative effect. And in fact, he was never mistaken about these purchases; everything he bought for his houses and which was sold at auction after his death fetched a good price, sometimes far beyond the real value."

Villa Fontanelle would be the triumph of neoclassical style. "Because neoclassical is the easiest door to enter in the antiques business," Baroni goes on. "It's a simple style, it makes a big statement, and in these years it was beginning to be fashionable in stylish homes. And Versace had a lot to do with making it fashionable. He was buying things in Milan, in Florence, in Rome. He was a particular kind of collector; he wanted to surround himself with beautiful things that pleased him, that spoke to him. For example, paintings by Luigi Ademollo, Francesco Hayez, Giuseppe Bezzuoli or Giovanni Migliara, whether large or small, with their air of longing for a Greek world of unattainable perfection, and their mostly male figures taking part in the pitched battles of the centaurs or in bacchanalian rites. But at Villa Fontanelle, Gianni also had two fine female figures sculpted of marble in 1830 by

Pompeo Marchesi, a leading Milanese sculptor and student of Canova. And he had a huge picture gallery covering every inch of the walls, mostly paintings from 1700 to 1800 of women in marvelous, sumptuous clothing by painters from Andrea Appiani to Giuseppe Bossi to Gaspare Landi."

Versace had a theater director's eye, a set designer's intuition. "When he bought something," says Baroni, "he already knew where he would put it and what effect it would have on that room. But even in this much-loved house of his, nothing was eternal. Gianni would continue to add new things: in a year the number of miniatures went from two to fifty; the shutters, white, were repainted in black; the silver oil lamps, a mere decorative element, although they were a genuine passon of his, multiplied almost indefinitely." The only thing that never changed was a Neapolitan *presepe*, an elaborate Christmas crèche of the 18th century, that was set up every Christmas in the ground floor drawing room.

"Villa Fontanelle was always Gianni's favorite house," says Giuseppe Menta. "When he could, he'd get there early, arriving on Thursday evening and then puttering around the house doing his favorite chores. For example, he would polish the picture frames with great care, with the love he felt for all his things. We had a house nearby at Cernobbio and we would pay him a visit on Sundays. We would talk, have lunch, be together." Even at the lake, however, Gianni was thinking about work. On Fridays, he might convene the makers of the printed silks he liked— Menta, Antonio Ratti, Enzo Tria, Michele Canepa and

Walter Ragazzi, who still produces Versace silk accessories. They would cover the floors of the studio, and the space under the magnolia tree by the lake outdoors, with the paper print samples they had brought to show him. They talked, debated and decided which of the several patterns was the best. And while they were doing this, the architect would sometimes be there making sketches for the carpenter who needed to remake a *boisierie*, or for the workman who was building a new ceiling or putting in a new floor. Versace loved to surround himself with imaginative, thoughtful people, from whom he'd get ideas, right down to the gardener who might have an idea on what color flowers would give a certain flower bed a lift. In this dimension, where work and leisure could flow together just as he pleased, he felt particularly comfortable.

"Gianni thought of Villa Fontanelle as his real home," says Menta. He spent every Christmas here, surrounded by his family, who served as his protection, his home side. His father Antonio always came, and his cousin Nora, and the two of them played cards in the library. His father didn't always feel at ease in the midst of those luxurious surroundings; once, when Gianni gave him his own bedroom to sleep in, wanting him to have the best room, Antonio was unable to sleep and asked for a more modest room for the rest of his visit. And then there were Donatella and Paul, with their children Allegra and Daniel, and Santo and his wife Cristiana with their children, Antonio and Francesca. Uncle Gianni had a special place in his heart for Allegra; he called her "my little princess" and loved to say to her, "Let's see you do Marpessa,"[1] while Allegra stalked seriously down the carpets of the ground floor drawing room. Gianni needed to have his family around him; a man of the South with an impetuous, sometimes tyrannical character, he also desperately needed an atmosphere of affection around him.

When it came to promoting his own brand, however, Versace was also an inspired public relations man on his own behalf. And Villa Fontanelle was a perfect showcase, a stage for certain business-related occasions, such as the launch of a new perfume, or a reception to thank the textile producers of IdeaComo for having awarded him a prize. Gianni alternated work-related receptions with parties for friends, like the one he held for numerous fashion people to celebrate the ninetieth birthday of the doyenne of Italian fashion journalism, Maria Pezzi.

"An evening I'll never forget was the housewarming for Villa Fontanelle," says Gianni Bertasso. "The villa was lit up day-for-night, and there were all the great first generation models—Jerry Hall, Kelly LeBrock, Rene Russo, Beverly Johnson, and so forth. From the lake, under a thundering downpour, came the local boats called the Lucie, filled with the young women of the lake chorus dressed in costume, singing. It was a magnificent, almost unreal, spectacle. Inside the house we could move around everywhere, even in the bedrooms. Everything was gorgeous, perfect, stunning. No doors were closed."

---

1. Marpessa was a particularly classy model of the period.

CHAPTER 7

1982: A Big Year

The eighties, decade of the climbers, the careerists, the brash. Hedonism as a way of life, the cult of the body, a new conservatism after the confrontational period of the 1970s, the desire to see and be seen. "Muscular" years, Emanuele Pirella, guru of the progressives in the PR world, dubbed them. "Years with no ideological or ethical foundation," the observer of manners Roberto D'Agostino put it. This was the decade of the *look*. It was a golden moment for Italian fashion; between 1971 and 1981, the number of clothing shops doubled and employment in the sector grew rapidly. The clothing business boasted a surplus of 11,000 billion lire, a sum that would have been more than enough to cover all of Italy's energy needs. And the trend would strengthen by the end of the decade. People wanted status symbols to show for their money, their success, their well-being. And sporting a label was the simplest way to announce one had arrived. The designers became stars. The champions of Italian Style, Armani and Versace, divided the territory. On one side, Armani perfected his conception of a woman linked to female liberation in the 1970s, creating the perfect image for the professional, the career woman.

On the other side, Versace was the great interpreter of the decade's drive for show, for appearances—linked, as always with him, to the eternal feminine.

"The woman he created is the one everyone is doing today," says Franca Sozzani, editor in chief of *Vogue Italia* since 1988, but familiar with Versace from the seventies, when she worked at *Lei*, the Condé Nast magazine for younger women. "Gianni was always something of an extremist, he was always making a statement, he always wanted to go beyond the canons of fashion. And yet he never fell into vulgarity, which is something you can't say about contemporary fashion, which has become a mass market phenomenon. Gianni, instead, represented an elite trend."

The late Richard Martin, influential director of the Costume Institute of the Metropolitan Museum of Art in New York, agreed. And he went even further: "Gianni Versace rewrote the criteria for showing off. He wasn't aiming at decorum, but wanted to align fashion with desire, substituting the sensuality of the clothes and the enjoyment of the body for such criteria as good manners and social importance." Furthermore, said Martin, "Nobody had ever brought the prostitute into fashion the way he did. In a feat worthy of literature, Versace seized the streetwalker's bravado and conspicuous wardrobe, along with her blatant, brandished sexuality, and introduced them to high fashion." Transforming and translating them. "Versace gave us the streetwalker as style," Martin went on. "He appropriated the extreme flirtation of the short skirts, the seductiveness of the shiny fabrics.... But in doing so, however, he didn't simply reproduce what you might find in a hooker's closet. He translated these elements, one by one, into hyperbolic, highly expressive versions." With his sensual drapery, the transparent lace, the glitter of chain mail, the luxury of the silk evening gown with the train, he created his "composite of Cinderella and Delilah." There was nothing there to please the establishment, who always regarded Versace with diffidence anyway, "keeping their distance from his targeted vulgarity and shameless enthusiasm for consumerism." For that matter Versace, although never rejecting the establishment outright, was always an outsider to it, both as a designer and as a person.

In 1982 Gianni Versace invented—and invented is the right word for it—a new material, chain mail, a sort of metal mesh. After having experimented with it in his medieval-look men's collection, with jackets in rust-iron color, he decided to try it out in the womenswear line that same season. He obviously couldn't use the same chain mail, for it was too heavy. He began to work on a metallic "knit" that would suit the female body. In just a few months, with the help of a German artisan, he invented Oroton: a fine chain mail made of metallic elements— minuscule rings of brass alloy for the silvery parts, aluminum alloy for the colored bits. Versace sent the first Oroton dresses out on the runway not at the old Milan Fair location where most fashion shows then took place, but in a one-man show on the third floor of Via della Spiga 25. The dresses were long slips tied at the waist with a sash, or simple tunics, and the new material was light and adhered closely to the body, picking up its heat. The spectators, invited 500 at a time for the three showings of the collection, were enthusiastic. From now on, Versace would show chain mail fabrics in each of his collections, reinventing the clothes continually, in cut and color as well as in the geometric patterning, and often adding sequins. Women who wore these clothes remember being almost embarrassed by the sexiness they emitted. Versace was very proud of this new fabric, telling André Leon Talley at *Vogue France*, "This chain mail is different from the metallic dresses created in the last decade by the followers of Paco Rabanne; it's not in any way aggressive or hard. It's not meant to be a shock factor for those who wear it, or for those who look at those wearing it. I certainly didn't create it to be used as a costume."

For his innovative and experimental collection, Versace won the Occhio d'Oro, a new prize for the top designer of the season just introduced that year and sponsored by Revlon. "Versace was a designer with technological flair," says Mario Boselli, chairman of the Chamber of Fashion and Industrial Textiles. "He was the only designer in the history of Italian fashion to create his materials *ex novo*. He didn't merely choose his fabrics, refine them, and put his stamp on them. He *invented* those fabrics. I remember the one we designed together at the end of the 1980s: we called it "Africa" and it's still in production. It started with a very fine strand of nylon, made by Marioboselli Jersey, that was twined during the production phase to a thread of viscose, that too made by us. The fabric that came out was silky, semi-shiny and washable, and it could be used just as it was. But the best part was still to come. If you took this jersey and you gave it a *devore* treatment, that is, if you corroded the viscose by chemical means, what you got—that is, the very fine worked nylon—allowed you to achieve a completely transparent fabric. Versace used this *devore* material to make extraordinary patterns, differing from one season to another, one time geometric, one time floral, one time mono-colored, another with overprints in various colors. A number of the clothes he designed in these fabrics are in museums today." Versace's technological prowess earned him a place as the only fashion designer invited to the È Design exhibit the following year at Milan's PAC contemporary art space.

A few days after the Milan show at which he introduced metal mesh, Gianni flew to Paris and then to America. He had by now overcome, at least in part, his fear of flying—a fear that at the beginning of his career meant that colleagues sitting next to him had to keep talking to him nonstop during the flight, an experience they recall with much warmth and tenderness. His destination was the Paris Opéra, that 19th-century temple of dance and operatic music so beloved by the French. It would be the first time that the Opéra opened its doors to a representative of fashion. The occasion was the introduction of a new Versace perfume, and the evening was one of those society events at which Parisians excel. The upper crust was there, along with stars of the cinema world and various ladies of style. They were celebrating the tenth anniversary of Versace's design with a multivision show of his fashions right up to the latest men's and women's collections. The evening then continued with a concert including pieces by Scarlatti and Vivaldi, and concluded with a playful touch: a group of mimes and acrobats in 18th-century costumes. Gianni was radiant; a photo shows him alongside the beautiful Michèle Mercier, star of *Angelica*, smiling and looking a bit shy.

Two months later in May, it was time for a visit to America. It wasn't Versace's first trip; he had been there in 1977 with one of the collections he was designing in that period, and Diana Vreeland had insisted upon following his show from backstage, so she could see how Gianni dressed the models and accessorized their clothes. But this time, it was to be a major visit. Italian journalist Elisa Massai, then working for the *Daily News* (and afterwards for *Women's Wear Daily*) wrote: "In these last few months, the Italian designer has crossed the ocean six times, and gone from New York to Palm Springs, from San Francisco to Los Angeles. On this trip he presented his 'best of' fashions already shown in Italy plus a small collection created ad hoc for American women (relying on Diana Vreeland's counsel). And finally, in a marvelous evening in Los Angeles full of glamour and personality, he gave a preview of his fall-winter 1982–1983 collection to the American press. Result: thunderous applause and crazed buyers, because more than the others this Italian designer, with his sexy, frothy and really very innovative clothes, is perfect for the American market." Crowning "the American tour of the genius Gianni Versace," as Massai put it, was the opening of the men's and women's boutique on Madison Avenue in Manhattan's elegant heart.

In that same year, Giorgio Armani saw himself featured on the cover of *Time* under the headline "Gorgeous George."

That March 1982 was truly a prophetic moment for Versace. For after he had presented his women's and then his men's collection for the fall-winter 1982–1983 season, all of a sudden, the theater world wanted him. La Scala asked him to design the costumes for the Richard Strauss ballet *Josephs Legende*, choreographed by Joseph Russillo with sets by painter Luigi Veronesi. Versace had very little time to create the costumes and so he leaned heavily on the styles he had sent out at his most recent shows. For Zobeide, wife of Potiphar (performed by Luciana Savignano) he began with an evening dress with an asymmetric hem over leggings, transforming the single strap holding up the bodice into a thick braid that twined down the arm in two strips of blue Lycra. For the costumes of Joseph's eleven brothers, he followed the style of the pullovers he had shown in the men's collection, working with asymmetry, and sometimes sending out the very clothes shown in the collection, because he had so little time to create new ones. Here's how Giusy Ferré of *L'Europeo* told the story of the opening night on March 19: "There are two ballets on the program this evening: *Sheherazade*, with its Orientalist fables and drama, and *Josephs Legende* by Richard Strauss on a theme that inspired Thomas Mann to write one of his greatest classics, *Joseph and His Brothers*. But the first ballet ends with the public jeers of a crowd bored by the tired-out choreography, and Versace, who is struck dumb with panic at this, his debut, thinks he has been foolish to take on such a challenge, from which he will surely emerge the loser. 'This is too much of a risk,' he says as he listens to the crowd's reactions. 'This isn't my world. I shouldn't have let myself be tempted.' "

Then the curtain went up on Veronesi's well-thought-out set, and all of a sudden Gianni felt an inner peace, an utter tranquility. "The costumes had an energy that matched the lights and the sets. The dancers moved with great discipline. It all seemed new to me, very modern. And so as I watched Luciana Savignano, I realized that the audience was going to be more generous with us." That evening, as the crowd at La Scala applauded enthusiastically and Russillo called him to the stage to join the curtain call, "Gianni Versace's impetuous and prolific love for the theater" was born, wrote the hard-to-please art critic Gillo Dorfles. "From that moment on, the designer would create dozens and dozens of costumes for each of the twenty ballets he would cooperate on with the masters of modern dance," added Dorfles, who credited Versace with exceptional bravura in the field. He wrote of "an extraordinary ability to interpret individual characters, in works from *Don Pasquale* to *Salomé* and *Dionysos*, from *Souvenir de Léningrad* to *Malraux ou La métamorphose des dieux*, while remaining true to the demands of the story, the action and the era—and yet creating fully invented costumes that take advantage of his design capacities, employing the costume as a function of the dance, and color as an aspect of the ballet's atmosphere."

That evening at La Scala would be a memorable occasion in Gianni Versace's private life, too. On that evening the designer met Antonio D'Amico. The handsome, dark haired young man worked as a salesman for a leather firm and another making knitwear—alternating these jobs with an occasional appearance as a runway model or in photos for magazine romance tales. Born January 21, 1959, in Mesagne, a small town near Brindisi in the southern Italian region of Puglia, Antonio had a mother who was a dressmaker, a father who died when he was young, an experience in boarding school, a decent stepfather and a diploma in hotel management. Antonio had been invited to La Scala by Carlo Belgir, an elegant gentleman who sold the must luxurious draperies in all of Milan and who liked to surround himself with attractive young men. "That evening, Carlo told me, there would be a ballet at La Scala with costumes by Versace," D'Amico recalls. "And that if I wanted to, we could attend. We went. After the performance, there was a first night dinner with all the artists: Russillo, Veronesi, the dancers, Versace. I'm introduced to him. As we're sitting down, Gianni tells me to sit near him. On the other side of the table was Gianni's partner at that time.

"I was delighted to be there, I had just seen a wonderful performance, but I felt a bit awkward in the situation, sitting right next to Versace, whom I considered

81

a genius of the fashion world. I was terribly excited and at the same time, I felt ill at ease. From time to time Gianni would get up to greet some of the guests, and many others came over to congratulate him. When the dinner was over Versace said goodbye to me and we exchanged phone numbers. He said, 'Maybe you'll come to dinner or to lunch at my studio.' But I didn't really expect anything; I had enjoyed the ballet and the evening and I went back happily to my little apartment in Piazza Cinque Giornate. A few days later, I was off for a tour in Japan with the operetta director Sandro Massimini. We were away for a month. When I got back, I turned on the answering machine and there were two or three calls from Gianni, and the last one said, 'This is the last time I'm going to call you.' I called him and said I was sorry, that I had been away for work. Gianni invited me to dinner at his home. He told me he had just broken up with his companion and that 'I thought of you. Even though you're quite a bit younger than I am, thirteen years younger, you seem like a steady person to me, someone with his head on his shoulders, a person of a certain maturity.' "

D'Amico pauses for an instant. He seems to be searching for the simplest, most accurate words to convey the emotion of that moment, so important in his life. "I was 23 years old. I was terribly flattered but I was also terrified. I had just broken off with a woman I worked with; she was older than I was and knew I was bisexual. It was a moment in which I just wanted to be free. Gianni began to court me; he invited me to dinner, to a weekend on Lake Como. He wanted me to be there for lunch at his office, where everyone treated me like a fish out of water and I felt somewhat embarrassed. We went on like that for a few months. I was cautious, and Gianni wanted me to be part of his world. Until one day he said, 'Why don't you come and work with me?' It meant a complete change of life for me. I thought about it for two months and then I said, 'Why not?' I had always wanted to move forward professionally, to grow. Gianni suggested I work in the sales office of Vesa, the company that managed Istante. And so I went to see his brother Santo Versace to be hired. He said to me, 'I don't know what kind of a relationship you have with my brother.' And I said, 'I don't think that's anything you need to concern yourself with.' And so he said, 'Okay, let's figure out your salary; you'll work for Istante.'

"But the job didn't work out. And so Gianni then suggested I could be his assistant for the theater. I loved the idea. And so it began: I would go to listen, first with him and then alone, to what the choreographers wanted; I would draw up the technical specifications for the dancers' roles, plan the work, and do research on materials to prep the assistant costumists who would draw the sketches. And then I would follow up on the costume production. Some were made in Novara, the leotards by Gadola, crinolines by Pai Rame, and other costumes were tailored by Tirelli Costumi. And that's when we began to live together. It was simpler that way, because Gianni always worked twenty-four hours out of twenty-four; he was always busy with something. In the evening at home, standing in his studio in his slippers, he would dash out quick sketches with a black felt pen, sketches that his assistants would transform into proper drawings."

Antonio got up and came back with some small black notebooks. On every page are hastily sketched drawings. And under each one, a few words in tailor's jargon: tailored suit with matching vest, shoulder pads, winter, sport, rustic, volume. He flipped through them as if they were works of art. "Or sometimes," he continued, "while I watched sports on TV Gianni would sit on a chair going through piles of newspapers and magazines. In the morning we got up early and each of us went our own way. After a few months, Santo came to me and asked me if I would come back to work at Istante. I said yes and I began to redesign the line under Gianni's supervision and with the help of the assistant designers."

That opportunity for a professional second chance is something Antonio is particularly proud of, obviously. It's the cue for him to begin to delve more deeply into his relationship with Gianni. "The tie between Gianni and me evolved day by day, growing more respectful, more affectionate. It became love after about a year and a half. We spoke about it a lot; we were conscious of being two men who had decided to be with each other, and it was important to maintain the consciousness we were men. We trusted each other, although we did sometimes have our moments of jealousy. I've never had a relationsip that was so intense. Gianni used to say to our common friends that I gave him equilibrium. There were never any huge fights, only those little quarrels that you find in all couples who get along; I used to reproach him for his messiness, or because I wanted to convince him to go to the gym. Only once did we ever have a real fight. There was a guy Gianni was involved with, a model; everybody knew about it. I went off by myself for a week; I didn't speak to him. And then Gianni came to me and told me he was sorry, and we got back together again. But I sort of kept my distance for two years; I made him feel insecure. From then on, our relationship became stronger."

In that same year, 1982, Antonio D'Amico also met Donatella Versace. "I met her almost right away, given that we were all there for lunch at one of the offices on Via della Spiga. She didn't like me: 'Okay, here's another one,' she thought. I liked her, instead, but I maintained a certain distance. With her husband Paul, though, I was quite friendly; he was a more easy-going kind of guy. Paul was the outsider who had found a family in the Gianni Versace firm. He and I were both outsiders. Toward Santo I felt very friendly. He seemed to me a little bit cut out of the relationship between Gianni and Donatella, because he didn't deal with design. However, family was family. The three siblings might go after each other like tigers, but when evening came, they were all united again. And it was Gianni who kept the family united, for family was all-important to him. The only exception he made was with Allegra, Donatella and Paul's daughter, to whom he'd give gorgeous presents. And I would remind him that there were also Daniel, and his other niece and nephew Francesca and Antonio, who were Santo and Cristiana's children."

CHAPTER 8
Béjart and Elton John

"The first contact between Béjart and me took place through our creations, almost exactly at the same time but in separate places": so Gianni Versace told the Sunday supplement of *Il Sole 24 Ore*. "Béjart, who was in Japan for a tour, had seen my pullovers from the Archeologia line with inserts based on details from Etruscan vases, in a boutique over there. I was in Florence, meanwhile, where I was bewitched by his *Trionfi* and his *Molière imaginaire*." It was as if the two great image-makers of the moment had looked at each other from afar, scrutinized each other and held each other in their ken, alert and ready to grab new ideas and invent more. As if they knew they were destined to meet, to create new ideas and give birth to new sensations. Marseille-born Maurice Béjart, real name Berger (his father was the philosopher Gaston Berger whose ideas on mysticism and on how the past relives in the present exerted a strong influence on his son's intellectual formation), had renamed himself Béjart in honor of a family related to Molière, the French playwright having been his first great passion as a boy. He was nineteen years older than Versace, and he was something more than just the choreographer who had staged hundreds of ballets set to all kinds of music—Bach and Chopin, Ravel and Kurt Weill, Wagner and Bartok, Beethoven and Schönberg, urbane contemporary scores—in all the leading theaters of the world. "With Béjart," wrote dance critic Vittoria Ottolenghi, "it wasn't just a question of matching dance to the demands of a world ruled by images, but of creating, almost in the very vitality of the act, images through the drive to dance. And this drive, this movement, these images, didn't come from fusing classical ballet and modern dance, but from fusing classical ballet and the content of modern dance." Past and present that wove together, pursued each other, combined. Just as in Versace's fashion.

Béjart—periwinkle blue eyes (the eyes of a medium, the legend went), a Mephistophelean face underscored by a sculpted little faun's beard—became Béjart in 1959 when he staged Stravinsky's *Rite of Spring*, and moved from a role as choreographer of single dancers to choreographer of entire ballets, giving male dancers back their dignity by creating a lot of space for them in his performances. He explained his new style of dance in a 1983 interview with *Danza & danza*. "I wasn't entirely convinced about the Stravinsky *Rite*," he said of his first reaction when the director of the Théâtre de la Monnaie, Maurice Huisman, proposed he do the ballet. "The *Rite* was written in 1913 and I thought I would be taking a step backward to follow that choreography. At the same time, Huisman needed something big to open his first season at the Théâtre de la Monnaie. I remember that I consulted the I Ching and the hexagram gave me the following

reply: 'sublime success thanks to the sacrifice of spring.' I
was floored. I couldn't refuse. I decided to say yes
immediately to Huisman's request and I asked him if I
could have the dancers of the Western Ballet and of the
Théâtre de la Monnaie for the performance, along with
the dancers of my own company Ballet-Théâtre. I wanted
to realize my dream: to let all the urgent desire explode in
a group choreography, to strip the *Rite of Spring* of every
scrap of historical and folkloric reference that was
damping down the value of that music. Out with the
Russian costumes, out with the primitive and all the
scenography that restricted the universal impact of
Stravinsky's score. In their place, groups of young men
and women in leotards (pale for the women; red, brown
and green for the men) that would underline the concept
of femininity and its exact opposite. I wanted to celebrate
beauty, youth, passion, sexual striving, eliminating any
esthetic modesty and above all, any pagan connotation.
The *Rite of Spring* must portray a contemporary religious
rite." You can almost hear Versace's clothes talking here.
The two met in real life in the spring of 1984, to stage
Dionysos. La Scala had commissioned Béjart to stage the
work the previous year, but it was postponed after the
choreographer had a bad fall during the rehearsals. But
now all was ready. *Dionysos* debuted in a world première
on June 8 at the Palasport arena in Milan with the dancers
of the Ballet du XX Siècle company.

What kind of ballet was *Dionysos*? Béjart himself—
somewhat reluctantly because he disliked talking about
his performances before the public had seen them—

explained his ideas at the press conference to present the ballet, as recorded by *la Repubblica*'s Leonetta Bentivoglio and *Epoca*'s Gabriella Monticelli. "Dionysus is the god who presides at the birth of dance, music and theater, and he is the Greek god who has always attracted me most. I know him above all through my reading of Nietzsche. Two cultural-historic stages meet in this performance, influencing each other reciprocally; the characters are Dionysus, the god of joy; Wagner and his wife Cosima; and Nietzsche. They represent the South and the North as they confront one another; Greece and Germany; past and present. The overall significance of this work lies in the resurrection of a civilization that has been destroyed. Dionysus is a great figure of myth; a very crazy, very violent, very modern way of being in the world. Nietzsche, remember, in the most extreme experience of his madness, identified with Dionysus, glorified Wagner, and fell in love with Cosima. On the stage we see two worlds: an ancient Greece of great military parades and costumes, and Wagner's drawing room. There is no precise narrative, just many symbolic frames; for example, we see the Nazis invade Greece and Wagner, dressed as a soldier, entering Athens on a tank. And in that same moment, we see Dionysus in a tavern.... The music is a melange, as in many of my other ballets: half are compositions by Wagner, from the *The Ring* to *Tannhäuser*, and the other half are works by the Greek composer Manos Hadjidakis, but the sound track also includes Indian and Byzantine music.

"As for the scenography, this time I don't use my preferred neutral backdrops. The sets are painted by the Japanese artist Yokoo Tanadori; costumes are by the designer Gianni Versace. I usually like to send the dancers on the stage in simple leotards, but many ballets need dress costumes, and some, like *Dionysos*, demand them. Versace has an extraordinary sense of movement and of dance."

All his bravura for mixing traditions and cultures were on show in Versace's designs for the costumes of *Dionysos*. His costumes were potent hybrids, as in that created for the Greek god, whose cult is apparently of oriental origin and whom Gianni imagined in red tights with fiery red layered trousers over them, a look borrowed from the designer's spring-summer 1982 women's collection and reworked to suggest traditional Balinese dancers' wear. Theater critic Mario Pasi describes this costume in a passage of his book *Versace teatro*, published by Franco Maria Ricci. "Gianni Versace imagines the god Dionysus in a pair of trousers that are half Greek, half Indian, bright red, and magically these trousers appear and even more magically engulf the legs of the demigod who can thus claim two civilizations in one go. And Maurice Béjart puts himself beside the son of Zeus and Semele—Dionysus— on the cart, and the two converse as if they had come together and become brothers in a very ancient time."

Versace, who was very much in his element in the world of Béjart's imagination, saw the Belgian choreographer as his "master of life and taste." "I owe him an immense debt," he told Vittorio Sgarbi and Fiona Diwan in *Grazia*. "I feel I am his ideal disciple. He has taught me what theater means: to dare the undareable, to put everything in question. Through him I have rediscovered my roots, the Mediterranean, Greece.... Wasn't I, after all, born in the heart of Magna Graecia, in Calabria, beside a temple, among mosaics, next to ancient stones that are full of history? I always feel love and gratitude to anyone who teaches me something I didn't know. I'm curious; I'm hungry to learn new things. They nurture my creativity."

The designer repaid the favor with unusual generosity. Béjart recalled that when they were preparing *Dionysos*, he would ask for ten sketches and Gianni would give him thirty or forty, "and if you want, we can do more," he'd say cheerfully. "Their connection went beyond business, beyond the commercial side," says Mario Pasi, who shared a real friendship with Béjart and Versace, as well as an interest in theater. "In his own way Gianni was an intellectual, and the theater was one of his passions. For his part, Béjart wasn't at all interested in fashion, nor did he see the theater as having anything to do with luxury. He was a regular at La Scala, and his yearly performances, produced in Brussels and in Lausanne, quickly became an integral part of the program at La Scala. Béjart offered Versace the chance to create his costumes in what was a very free work relationship. They met and they liked each other right away. They had two things in common: a love for classical culture—in Béjart's case, Greece, and in Versace's case Magna Graecia, for he was very attached to his origins—and a taste for contemporary music. Béjart always used, as part of his sound track, not only the classics, but pop-rock groups, from the famous, like Freddy Mercury and Queen (to whom he dedicated the ballet *Le presbytère*) to little-known groups. And Versace was friends with Sting and Elton John."

Maurice Béjart remembered Gianni and their connection fondly. "Working with Gianni was a joy—the joy of friendship and the joy of creativity. Work, I believe, is that place where everything converges and joins together in the finished piece. Gianni did not devour, he didn't take; he lent esthetic, spiritual and spatial depth to a character. It's very rare to work with someone who reflects your own competence, and who at the same time is able to offer so much wealth in terms of images and ideas. In every moment Versace was novelty, wonder, an uninterrupted flow of ideas."

The pas de deux between Béjart and Versace had just begun. It would go on for thirteen years, until the designer's death, with a few side steps by Versace, who would also design costumes for several productions by Robert Wilson. But the most successful partnership was always that between the man from Calabria and the man from Marseille. Two years after *Dionysos*, the two were at the Cirque Royal in Brussels to stage *Malraux ou La métamorphose des dieux*, with passages by Beethoven and traditional and oriental music by Hugues Le Bars. The ballet traced the work and thought of the 20th-century French philospher, illustrated in scenes that shifted in time from Chiang Kai-shek's Nationalist China to the Nazi concentration camps to the Resistance, to freedom. Béjart wanted to stage it in black and white. Versace designed sophisticated, sumptuous costumes inspired by the haute couture of the past—from Madeleine Vionnet's extraordinary bias cuts of the 1920s, to Madame Grès and her wonderful draped styles, right down to Coco Chanel and her bathing costumes for classy holidays at Deauville. The costumes were so beautiful that many critics saw them as the high point of the performance.

"Versace made many very elaborate costumes based on luxurious and costly materials," Mario Pasi recalls. "The dancers, behind the scenes, treated them like ordinary costumes, dragging them across the floor without paying attention. Gianni would run after them, begging them to be more careful." According to fashion historians Nicoletta Bocca and Chiara Buss, the costumes he made for this performance marked a change in Versace's relationship to the theater. "The designer, who had previously brought his fashion ideas to the stage, began to do the opposite: he took what he had learned from his studies for the costumes and he applied it to some of the clothes in his collections. It was a signal that his relationship with Béjart had transformed the theater jobs into something engaging, creative and capable of donating new ideas to Versace's fashion work." The influence went even deeper. "With the costumes for *Malraux* Versace moved toward a fresh encounter with French couture of the twenties and thirties, a move that would deeply influence the development of his fashion and of the Versace Couture line."

In all this, nevertheless, Gianni had to struggle, he had to insist, in order to pursue his ambitions in the theater. So he explained in his conversation with Vittorio Sgarbi and Fiona Diwan in *Grazia*. "The theater," said Versace, "rewarded me with great creative freedom, a chance to try out new formulas and an energy that later showed up in my collections. For me it is a sort of workshop, a reservoir of ideas that I know will sooner or later end up in my fashion. Because theater is disguise; it's the art of veils and dressing up, it is fiction that becomes reality. Fashion is like that, too. At first it was very difficult for me to convince my family—my brother Santo and my sister Donatella. They didn't even want to hear the word theater. They said it would sap my energy, rob it from the business and the market. But for me, theater is a unique creative laboratory."

Over the years Versace would create thousands of costumes for the ballet, travelling back and forth across the centuries and around the world in search of inspiration. From *Salomé*, with Herodias's black dress like a whorl of petals that quoted an Elsa Schiaparelli style of the 1940s; to *Souvenir de Léningrad*, in which Béjart prophetically put Lenin on the stage in a scene dancing with the Czar while the revolutionaries looked admiringly at a statue of Peter the Great (and where Versace offered costumes on Constructivist motifs); to *Java Forever*, in which Zizi Jeanmaire wore a costume of jet-black beads and colored sequins that Versace showed again in the fall-winter 1989–1990 collection. And he would continue to draw inspiration from the ballet.

"For Versace," writes Roy Strong, art historian and director of the Victoria and Albert Museum, in the second volume of Franco Maria Ricci's *Versace teatro,* "designing costumes for the stage is an activity that would bring him international renown. He and the others involved know that they must maintain their equilibrium in a complex marriage of the arts. He would be the first to acknowledge that some of these marriages were more successful than others.... As far as I'm concerned, there's no doubt that his most successful collaborations were those with Maurice Béjart. His ballets are ideal vehicles for that amalgam of stunning performance and love of the bizarre and the fantastic that, although they sometimes involve a voyage into the past, are always part of any avant-garde." Béjart remembered Gianni Versace at work backstage: "On the eve of every first night, in the most unexpected cities, I would find Gianni Versace at work finishing and perfecting the marvelous costumes he had invented.... Watching him work enchanted me: he would be there sewing pearls on a dress, painting on golden embroidery, cutting out pieces of transparent silk, attaching invisible bits of lace in the folds of a costume where they were so hidden that only he and I knew they were there. But in the composition of a work of art, it is precisely what you don't see that makes something a masterpiece: it's the pointless that is absolutely indispensible. Gianni would sew quickly and methodically and that told me that an artist is first and foremost a great craftsman, and a craftsman a thinker who is both meticulous and insatiable."

Gianni Versace also had another close friendship in the performance world, with Elton John, the famous pop-rock singer. Reginald Kenneth Dwight (his real name) was close to being Versace's exact contemporary; he was born in Middlesex, England, in 1947. Before he became a pop star, Elton had been something of a boy wonder. By the age of 11 he was an accomplished pianist and had won a scholarship to the Royal Academy of Music. Although he cultivated his enormous talent, he was ever more drawn to popular music like rock and the blues, which he began to study alongside the classics. Ten years later, just 21 years old, he had his first success with "Your Song," followed by such evergreens as "Rocket Man," "Daniel" and "Island Girl." He was a star, crowned with gold and platinum records, sold-out concerts and crazed fans. Gianni Versace, who loved rock music, knew these Elton John hits from the seventies and he used them as a sound track for his fashion shows. His first meeting with the singer took place in 1986, a few years after he had met Béjart. Once again, it was fashion that brought the two stars together. Elton John was a regular at Versace's boutiques, beginning with the one in London. He bought entire male collections sight unseen, and sometimes jewelry, for he loved necklaces and had a vast collection of Victorian brooches.

"One day he came to Milan and asked to meet Versace in the store," Antonio D'Amico recalls. "Gianni, Paul Beck and I went to meet him and we stayed to help him with his purchases. The boutique was closed all afternoon. And he and Gianni struck up a real friendship right away." Elton John hadn't yet emerged from his worst days, marked by depression and cocaine use. The English tabloids went after him for years with scandal after scandal, some of them true but also often invented. Compulsive shopping for clothes (and for lots of other things) was probably one of his ways of dealing with unhappiness and a sense of emptiness. Elton John actually confided in Gianni Versace that very afternoon. D'Amico still remembers the occasion: "Elton, as Gianni would later tell me, bared his soul to Gianni. He was aware that he had so much—so much talent, so much wealth—but he felt unhappy, he was unable to find a longterm partner, something he deeply wanted. And he hated not being physically handsome. He was very open, very human, with Gianni, because obviously he felt he could trust him. And Gianni 'fell in love,' you might say, with him."

Thus the friendship between Gianni Versace and Elton John—based on an affinity of character and the generous spirit they shared—was born, and it would only grow stronger. They also shared a lot of fun. "They would talk several times a week," says Patrizia Cucco, who joined Versace as his personal assistant in 1985. "Elton John would call Versace from wherever he was around the world and the two of them would joke on the phone like two children. Both Gianni and Elton had a great sense of humor." They also went shopping together, buying everything from clothes to furniture to antiques. Elton felt close to Gianni, as if he were family, and came to stay at Villa Fontanelle happily, although he rarely liked to visit anyone. He also began to be interested in the home and decorating, inspired by what he seen of the homes of his friend. In Venice, Gianni took Elton to the shop of the famous Olga on the island of Burano, where he got him to buy beautiful antique lace tablecloths. Elton in turn took Gianni to the island of Murano where he introduced him to the great glassmakers Venini and Seguso and Barovier, and turned Gianni on to handmade glass. A few years later, Versace signed a contract with Venini to produce glassware for his Home Collection.

In 1989 Elton John, debilitated by hypertension and stress, passed out on the stage during a concert in Paris. "For Elton, it was the last chapter in a lifetime of living dangerously, and from then on he would slowly try to get back to normality," wrote Cristina Gabetti in *Marie Claire*. He appeared in public again in 1993 with a world tour and the album *The One*, including the moving "The Last Song" dedicated to a young man with AIDS whom the singer, along with the man's family, looked after right to the end. "What did you learn from that experience?" Gabetti asked Elton John. "I learned a stronger sense of reality, to put the right value on things. Once I used to complain about everything and it took nothing at all to irritate me—it might be the color of the hotel suite or the private airplane on which we were travelling. Seeing those people face a challenge of that kind in such an impressive way gave me a shock, as if I'd suddenly woken up." Gianni Versace designed the cover for *The One*, and he presided over his friend's triumphant return to the stage and to life. Gianni also designed the sets for that tour—a giant spaceship—and the costumes for Elton, the musicians and the singers.

"Nothing too bizarre," he said, "because he loves classic clothes and orders them by the dozens in different colors, all the same cut. He likes to have fun overloading them with accessories, sexing them up with small details, wearing them with wild and crazy hats."

CHAPTER 9
Recognition

By the mid-1980s, Gianni Versace was one of the shining
stars of Italian fashion. His costumes for the ballets of
Maurice Béjart and Robert Wilson had put a touch of
glamour on stages around the world. And his fashion,
influenced by his close relationship with the theater, had
become more "cultivated." In his fall-winter 1984–1985
collection, Versace drew on avant-garde art for his
inspiration, in two different ways. He created a series of
evening dresses based on Picasso's Cubist paintings, not
merely drawing on the motifs, but actually trying to
reproduce the artist's breakdown of the spatial dimension
in the structure of the clothes. And then he took the
liberty of doing exactly the opposite: picking up Vasily
Kandinsky's abstract patterns and translating them into
pure graphic decorative motifs. He would do the same
thing the following year drawing on themes by Kolo
Moser and the Viennese Secession, and with drawings by
Gustav Klimt that he reproduced on his chain mail, now
more sumptuous than ever, with trimmings in tiny glass
beads. In fall-winter 1986–1987, the collection focused on
the Optical look, based on the work of Hungarian artist
Victor Vasarely, and here Versace's bravura lay in his use

of black-and-white patterns that expanded and shrank, emphasizing the shape of the body. His virtuoso talent seemed to know no limits. And so it was no surprise that a distinguished instituiton like the Victoria and Albert Museum wanted to bring Versace into its hallowed halls as an exemplar of contemporary fashion.

The museum's director, Roy Strong, had become a close friend of Versace, counseling him on the design of his garden at Villa Fontanelle. Now he decided he wanted Londoners to see the designer's creations firsthand. Along with Italian art historian Rosa Maria Letts, Strong organized a two-day conference entitled "Versace, an Artist in Fashion." Reporting for *Corriere della Sera*, Adriana Mulassano wrote of the event: "Before a very smart audience (in the front row were Prince and Princess Michael of Kent) seated in the marvelous gallery of the Raphael Cartoons, Gianni Versace sent out his finest work of this year: two fall-winter collections that have already been seen and two as yet unveiled (spring-summer 1986 which will show at Milano Collezioni next year), timed to the music of Vivaldi and coming to a conclusion with the ravishing image of a dark bride, as mysterious and compelling as if she had emerged from a painting by Goya." Among the many evening dresses, black and white predominated, along with the famous chain mail dresses. But what made Versace's appearance in the British capital really special was the lecture he delivered the day after the gala, to an audience of 450 students of design and art from around the country. In the morning, the students heard talks by Valerie Mendes, the V&A's curator for clothes and textiles (her department had just received a donation of designs by Versace), and Rosa Maria Letts, who situated Versace in Italian art history with particular reference to Renaissance painting.

In the afternoon, Versace himself appeared before the crowd of aspiring young artists and designers, their hair dyed punk pink and orange, their minds quick to absorb the new, their notebooks at the ready. As Versace spoke, he explained the philosophy behind his fashions, but also much more. Showing them patterns and sketches, he illustrated the technical skills he used to give his clothes their unmistakable style. His lecture focused on three concepts. The first: the necessity for a fashion designer to be aware of his or her own traditions, "because it is only with knowledge of the past that one can have the confidence to approach the present and the future." Secondly, he advised, "follow and try to understand the new artistic trends and philosophic currents of your time, even those that seem unappealing, in order to perceive how fashion will evolve." And then, "when you are designing an item of clothing, you must never forget to think about its wearability and the use it will be put to, because there is no alternative to the combination beauty-utility in making good clothes." But where the students became genuinely enthusiastic was when Versace, patterns and fabrics in hand, explained: "A good design must begin with the materials. I suggest that you coordinate your fabrics with your sketches, your colors, your cuts, your buttons—in effect, with your style. No ready-made fabric can be made into something new, something of yours. If I want to make a tweed my own, I must work on the thread, the colors, and the weaving process. This is what I do for the fabrics I use. The more a print pattern is your own, the more the shape you give the clothing will belong to you too. The more a color is the one you have invented, the closer you will be to the garment you want. You must not leave a single belt or a single button to chance if you want a style to be your own."

Eagerly asking questions, the students seemed electrified by Versace's remarks. He concluded with some advice: "You can never have enough experience and your ideals will always outpace you. I remember that when I was just starting out and full of enthusiasm, everything seemed possible; I wanted to break the rules, mix up the cuts, use unheard-of fabrics and materials that had never been seen together. But don't think it was easy to get manufacturers and technicians to do what I wanted, to make something that hadn't been seen before. Above all I had to win their confidence and that took time—while I wanted to do something new and I wanted to do it right away. Your politeness, respect and patience for those who know less than you do has to be equal to that you have for those who know more than you do." When he finished, the students stayed to ask questions and talk with him all afternoon. For Flavio Lucchini, then editor in chief of *Donna*, the lecture at the V&A was unforgettable. "I was listening to Gianni Versace give an entire lecture in English; he must have learned it very fast but he was fluent. I was astonished: here was this autodidact from deepest Calabria, speaking English in London. He was an enormous success because he knew how to transmit his enthusiasm to others as nobody else could."

Versace's lecture at the London museum testified to the Calabrian designer's great talent. But it was also a signal that Italian fashion, in full flower in the mid-1980s, was now worthy of serious attention. The art world thus paid homage to fashion, it celebrated its creative energy and the fascination of the "look." Milan's cultural intelligentsia—artists like Emilio Tadini and Enrico Baj and architects like Gae Aulenti—created posters and billboards for the Modit ready-to-wear shows at the Milan Fair. Painter Renato Guttuso offered his friend Nicola Trussardi the drawings of his beloved sunflowers and corn cobs so that the designer could make floaty silk blouses. Internationally celebrated writers were happy to be invited by Krizia—who in the meantime had become a partner in the feminist publishing house La Tartaruga—to present their books in the designer's townhouse on Via Manin. In the zeitgeist of the eighties, it was not by chance, suggests the art historian and astute observer of manners Gillo Dorfles in his book *La moda della moda* (*The Fashion of Fashion*), that fashion was truly the most fashionable thing around.

Only a few months later, even Italian politics got on board. The President of the Republic opened the doors of the Quirinale Palace in Rome to fashion trend-setters "with a glamorous reception for 350 people, as stylish and animated as the palace's seasoned functionaries could remember any time in the last twelve years," wrote Laura

Laurenzi in *la Repubblica*. And President Francesco Cossiga decorated seven fashion designers: Valentino got the highest honor, Cavaliere di Gran Croce; Giorgio Armani was named Grande Ufficiale; and Paola Fendi, Krizia, Wanda Ferragamo, Gianfranco Ferré and Gianni Versace were named Commendatore. After the ceremony, Versace declared, "I'm very happy. And I really like the fact there's this atmosphere of harmony among us designers. Although it also makes me laugh a little and I can't quite get out of my mind the traditional image of the *commendatore* as an old, fat guy." Loris Abate, president of the Chamber of Fashion and the man behind the awards ceremony, thanked Cossiga with a speech recalling that fashion was the Italian economy's second locomotive, just behind tourism. Fashion, said the President of the Republic, was "made of art, imagination and entrepreneurship." And as glamorous models flitted by wearing the fashions of the designers at the ceremony, Cossiga added that "we all know that behind the paillettes there are often so many sacrifices."

Sacrifices? Yes, indeed. "To say that Gianni Versace's workdays were intense is an understatement," says Patrizia Cucco. "He would arrive in the office at nine a.m., always very punctual. And he would leave at six-thirty, except for the three crazy days before the fashion shows. He always knew the evening before what his appointments would be the next day. I would note them down myself on a piece of paper that he put in his pocket and took home. At the beginning of the workday, he invariably had a meeting with his 'kids,' the young people from the style department, not more than eight of them, his pupils. Gianni would come in a with a bunch of sketches he had made at home and he would divide them up among the young designers according to their 'specialization.' But in fact all the young people were interchangeable; they all took part in the final project and they were all very involved; it was really a choral work. Then his appointments would begin. The most demanding time was when they would try on the samples: the partly made up clothes would come in from Alias, the manufacturer, and he would try them on models in the presence of the designer responsible for that item and the representative from the fabrics department, and they would decide on the cut, the length, the color. The one in charge was Franca Biagini, the head fitter, who was a sort of supreme judge. It was she who decided how many layers of padding were needed if Gianni wanted the shoulders emphasized in a certain way, how long a zipper should be, what the detail on a neckline would look like, how the stitching should be done. It was she who, if she saw that Gianni was uncertain about the length of a skirt, would make up three lengths, short, medium and long, so that he could decide. She was the omnipresent and irreplaceable technician who was more of a perfectionist than Gianni himself, and he was a maniacal perfectionist.

"And after that you might have some important person come in; it might be Robert Wilson coming to talk to Gianni about the costumes for *Salomé*. And then around one we would always break for lunch. While we were working at Via della Spiga, we all ate together in the big dining room next to the kitchen, where Alba, the cook, made wonderful pasta dishes with vegetables and the apple and carrot cakes that Gianni loved. Simple food. Gianni loved to sit at the table with all of us from the different departments, with a journalist who had been invited, the choreographer who was working with him on a ballet, or the actress whose look he was dedicating himself to. He was shy, but he loved to laugh and joke around. Then, when he shifted the offices to Via Gesù, he would eat lunch upstairs in his living space where a wonderful couple, Gianni and Lucia, looked after him. In the afternoon, Gianni would look over the work that had been assigned, or give interviews, or he would sit next to me and listen in on the phone calls, or maybe go by to see what bindings and trimmings Biagini had chosen. There was never a dull moment, never a break, but it was exciting, you felt you were taking part in something important. Gianni would also burst out in rages sometimes, when there was something he didn't like. But he hated to see people looking gloomy around him; he insisted that you pretend nothing had happened. Later, however, he would apologize in his way; he would toss out a joke, he would laugh about it, or sometimes the next day he would say he had changed his mind. If he went out and did some antiques shopping he would always come back with the image of a vase, a color or a motif that he would then translate into the design of his clothes. I've never seen anyone who was in love with his work the way he was."

And he was getting results. In 1985 sales for the Versace group reach 390 billion lire, a very healthy sum that included men's and women's ready-to-wear, the royalties due to Versace for lending his name to perfumes and accessories, his consulting fees for work with Genny, with the leather producer Mario Valentino, and others. "And we showed a 30 percent growth in sales compared to the previous years, as well as doubled our profits," said Santo Versace, adding that the group prospered "where the brand image maintained its distinction in the more than one hundred boutiques around the world under the supervision of architects Rocco Magnoli and Lorenzo Carmellini, following Gianni's lead."

In February 1986 Versace concluded a deal to buy one of Milan's most opulent residences, Casa Rizzoli at Via Gesù 12, once upon a time a home to princes and Lombard bankers, then, in the 1950s, to Angelo Rizzoli, chief of Italy's popular publishing house Rizzoli, and to his troubled and divided family. In 1981 Versace had already bought a first part of the house, an apartment of some 1,800 square meters where he was living. And at the same time he had also purchased the ground floor of the left wing where he installed his first offices, designed by Magnoli and Carmellini. Now, when Andrea Rizzoli, son of the founder, wanted to liquidate his estate, Versace concluded the purchase of the remaining 2,400 square meters plus the semi-underground floor and a garden with a beautiful *limonaia*. He paid a total of 14 billion lire for the house, and would spend some 6.25 billion to rehab and finish it. As Krizia had done with her townhouse on Via Manin and Giorgio Armani with his rather grander mansion on Via Borgonuovo, Versace used the three-story house to create his headquarters: offices, reception rooms, his atelier, and later, a theater for his fashion shows carved out of a temporary structure in the garden. He would be living over the shop as it were—in the greatest of luxury, of course. It was his own royal palace, and buying it made him proud and happy.

He redesigned everything except for the friezes in the great rooms on the second floor. Although he knew there was nothing very special about those friezes, he couldn't bring himself to remove them because they were installed when the Rizzoli family moved in and they seemed to him to be the soul of the house. But all the rest would be redone. In the half-basement, a team of young architects led by Gianfranco Cavaglià took down the old theater designed by the architectural firm Castiglioni, to make space for a swimming pool and gym. Versace wanted his office, the library, the style department and the fabrics department on the ground floor. His private apartment would occupy the entire first floor, and Versace supervised the design and decor himself with the help of the most celebrated architect-interior decorator of the day, Renzo Mongiardino, creator of striking, luxurious interiors. Marisa Rusconi, writing in *L'Espresso*, described him: "Architect, decorator, set designer, Mongiardino is above all the perfect esthete, a man in love with the past. Not because he wants to make of the past a place of frozen memory and nostalgia, but to recreate it in the present, defying the canons of a misunderstood and overly homogenized modernism." He could not have found a more sympathetic match in Gianni Versace, with his strong attachment to the past and his constant effort to remodel it and project it toward the future. "Recreating the perfect atmosphere has always been Mongiardino's goal—or perhaps one should say his obsession. Perhaps because he was surrounded by a fascinating mix of lines, colors and materials right from his early childhood in the aristocratic Genoese household into which he was born in 1916."

Mongiardino had gotten a degree in architecture from the Milan Polytechnic where he studied with the famous modernist Giò Ponti, and "already at the beginning of the 1950s his interest in classicism and a simplified architectural language that would hark back to great Renaissance architects like Alberti and Palladio, had found an outlet in his plans for several houses and shops in Milan." Mongiardino quickly became the interior designer favored by the great Italian industrial dynasties: the Crespi family, the Agnelli family, the Camerana, the Bonomi. And he soon moved beyond national boundaries to work for many big names in high finance and the jet set—the Rothschilds, the Kennedys, Onassis and Niarchos—as well as among artists, Franco Zeffirelli, to name just one. Soon he was working at the four corners of the Earth "followed by a troupe of painters, printers, mosaicists, lighting artists, pyrographists who would have been capable of satisfying the caprices and megalomanias of Holy Roman Emperor Rudolf II, or King Ludwig of Bavaria, but led by a chief artist, himself, so charismatic and so authoritative that he could control and channel those caprices and megalomanias." And Mongiardino also made a name for himself in the theater, designing the sets of Franco Zeffirelli's famous *Tosca* with Maria Callas at Covent Garden as well as sets for Zeffirelli's film of *The Taming of the Shrew*, for which he got an Oscar nomination.

Gianni Versace could not have chosen anyone else to decorate his house. And so Mongiardino reworked, to meet Versace's taste, the marble and wooden intarsia of the floors, the fabrics and frescoes on the walls, the cashmere upholstery, the mahogany window frames. And wherever genuine materials could not be found, he brought in artisans who could make amazing imitations. The interiors of Versace's apartment on Via Gesù, with all the objects collected by the designer, would make up the catalogue of an extraordinary museum. The entry hall, painted with trompe l'oeil columns, with its heavy silver chandelier, its 17th-century coin cabinet and its four headless statues. The drawing room, laid out like a Renaissance piazza, framed by four tufa stone columns from ancient Roman villas near Pompeii, pale beige tinted walls and a rare collection of Italian *veduta* paintings by Ippolito Caffi. From the other entryway with its Greek amphora in terra cotta (not hollow but solid because it was created to be a decorative piece), one passed into the reading room, decorated with a series of Greek and Roman heads, among them Dionysus, and then for a change of mood, two large 17th-century caricatures, paintings of the "silly emperors." The studio was lined with 16th-century Flemish paintings; the dining room with still lifes from the same period. Crowning the bedroom was a Florentine Renaissance baldachino, and the walls were decorated with paintings of the Via Crucis (the complete series of the stations of the cross), and many versions of the martyrdom of Saint Sebastian, his torso pierced with arrows. By the bedside stood a fragment of a Hellenistic statue of an adolescent, and on the headboard, painted ivory depictions of episodes in the life of King Charles I, decapitated by the English parliament in 1649. Versace insisted on his own design only for one room—his bathroom. He wanted a Roman bath in beige marble, the tub at floor level, with *grisaille*-painted walls depicting neoclassical figures. Mongiardino did it just as he wanted it.

International success had now arrived for Versace. And 1986 closed with a public tribute that marked another important stamp of approval for the designer. Paris, the city where fashion was born and from which it spread throughout the world; Paris, city of chic and grandeur where Versace went for work at least twice a year and stayed at the Ritz in the Windsor Suite, named for the Duke and Duchess of Windsor—Paris invited him to Palais Galliera, the Musée de la Mode et du Costume, for a show. It was called "Gianni Versace, Fashion Dialogues: Photographers and the Creation of a Style" and it was an exhibit in which all the photographers who had worked with him capturing images of his clothes and accessories both in advertising and in fashion magazine spreads, talked about working with Versace. There was Richard Avedon, king of glamour, whom Versace had selected for his ad campaigns back in the 1970s and who would work for him for twenty years; there was Helmut Newton with his supremely sexy images; there was the elegant Irving Penn; there were David Bailey, Gianpaolo Barbieri, Bruce Weber, Giovanni Gastel. "For the first time, Paris pays tribute to an Italian designer," wrote Laura Dubini in *Corriere della Sera*. Just one Italian before him had been an honored guest at the important Photography Month restrospective of which this show was a part. And that Italian was named Federico Fellini.

The show focused on the relationship between Versace and the photographers he commissioned. And the curators concluded: "A work on commission invariably involves a confrontation, a dialogue. In the case of Gianni Versace, his originality lies in his immediacy, in the fact there is no go-between. It is he and he alone who meets the photographer, who bargains with him, concedes, agrees, or rejects." It's not something we would ever really doubted.

In the crowning moment of the event, Prime Minister Jacques Chirac awarded Versace the Grande Médaille de Vermeil of the city of Paris, which had been given to just four Italians before him: Fellini, Luciano Pavarotti, soprano Renata Tebaldi and Franco Zeffirelli. Chirac praised Versace as "a humanist, an artist who creates in order to glorify the beautiful for his contemporaries." But the most heartfelt comment on Versace's work came from veteran fashion journalist Hebe Dorsey, fashion editor of the Paris-based *International Herald Tribune*. "Gianni Versace has been part of my professional life for such a long time that I have to make an effort to go back in memory to those long-ago years. However, I do remember when he showed his work at Palazzo Strozzi in Florence at the dawn of Italian prêt-à-porter, a dark moment for Italian fashion despite the marvelous fabrics, the fine quality of the leather and the unparalleled accessories, when there were, however, no really original designers.... At the time I was the only international fashion editor who attended those shows and year after year I kept coming back, always hoping for a miracle. I never lost my faith that sooner or later something would happen at those shows, even though they seemed so provincial. And so it did. Versace was the first to emerge with an original style, a real Italian style. He was the first ray of light. Not long after him, there were others. By now, Italian ready-to-wear had been born.

"In the course of his career and in my relations with him, which have inevitably become closer and more friendly, Versace himself has never changed. In terms of how he looks, I remember he always had that beard, the beard that makes him look like a classic bust of a Roman emperor, in that style that means so much to him.... Versace has always been somewhat reserved. He's a little bit nervous whenever he brings out a new collection. But he has always had an ideal he wants to promote and a fire inside that drives him along. His concept of a woman is very precise and he makes it concrete by using every means of seduction. Versace is the only Italian designer who makes clothes that are both sexy and witty.... All the same, I would never have imagined what refined taste he has in art, music and antiques. To visit one of his many homes, for example the villa on Lake Como or his princely headquarters in Milan, is to get to know a man of an unusual sensibility. How a young man of modest origins in Calabria came to assimilate, process and realize so much in so little time remains a mystery to me. And now it seems he has a new passion—fashion is no longer enough for him. What he really likes to do, what he does with great joy and peace, is to make the stage costumes for La Scala in Milan or for the Opéra in Paris.... It's hard to believe that Gianni Versace is only 39 years old."

CHAPTER 10
Money!

It was true: Gianni Versace, at 39, was already a success. But he didn't stop there. He couldn't stop. Not only because fashion is by definition change, and every designer must respect fashion's genetic code, creating something new, day after day. That was true for Versace, but there was more to it than that. His curiosity, his cultural hunger, his desire and ability to interpret the symbols of past and present, meant that he had no choice but to continually broaden his range of activity. The theater was one of his passions. After his encounter with Béjart, who remained his strongest point of reference in the field, Versace also worked with other artists. One of them was Robert Wilson, for whom he designed the costumes for the opera *Salomé*, from the play by Oscar Wilde and with music by Richard Strauss, which they would stage at La Scala in January 1987. The following year he would work with Wilson on his *Doktor Faustus*.

In June 1987 he was working once again with Béjart, creating the costumes for the Russian tour of his Ballet du XX Siècle, which culminated in a mega-performance seen on TV around the world, the *White Night of Dance*. He also did costumes for the ballet *Souvenir de Léningrad,* with the new company Béjart Ballet Lausanne. And he met Roland Petit, a master of classical choreography who was an expert at grafting popular dance styles onto the academic tradition. In January 1988 he created costumes for Petit's *Java Forever*, the last ballet to be performed by Zizi Jeanmarie, the choreographer's wife and a sophisticated dancer much beloved of the existentialists, who was bidding farewell to the stage. A few days later, his creations were once again onstage, this time at the Teatro Nazionale in Milan, where his longtime friend, singer Ornella Vanoni, wore costumes he had designed to harmonize with sets by artist Arnaldo Pomodori. That month of feverish activity for Versace closed in Sydney, Australia, at a huge show for the country's bicentennial taking place at the Opera House.

Versace's fashion was now moving swiftly in the direction of a more elegant and patrician woman. And in fact it was in 1987 that Versace launched his exclusive Couture line for women, three months after he had introduced the same idea for menswear. Interviewed by Marisa Rusconi of *L'Espresso*, the designer said, "I wanted to make clothes that are as close as possible to high fashion, that is to say, very carefully constructed and finished by hand, but I decided to focus only on daytime wear, on clothes dedicated to the active, successful working woman." The driving idea behind the new collection was already visible in the fall-winter 1987–1988 collection, where the tailored suit prevailed—a suit à la Versace, however, which included, yes, impeccable jackets perfect for high-powered women executives, ever so slightly spruced up with unusual closures or stoles made of the same fabric to toss casually around the neck. But also with enfant terrible skirts, incredibly short, with crazy pleats or irregular hems, or draped or held up with a bow on one side. In their book *L'abito per pensare* (*Fashion for Thought*), Nicoletta Bocca and Chiara Buss record what Versace told *la Repubblica*'s Silvia Giacomoni at the time: "The miniskirt is a fact of street fashion; you can't argue with it. And I was very certain I wanted short skirts because they are younger, more dynamic, freer and more modern. There's no going back: you'll see this winter. Only 30 percent of my Italian clients—I mean the shop owners—took to this idea of mine. All the rest of them were afraid and now they're shortening their skirts because that's how women want them."

The following season brought another surprise, when Versace introduced a long, clinging jacket that emphasized the curves of the female body, and another that was constructed like an elegant man's shirt—black, preferably—with sleeves that rolled up to just below the elbow. The idea was to provide women with a basic item of clothing for their well-tended wardrobes, yet also something that could keep up with the accelerated pace of modern life, that could meet the need to look perfect in the evening without changing from one's daytime clothes. He baptized this new look "blady," a cross between "blazer" and "lady" that he coined with semiotician Omar Calabrese. "Why me?" Calabrese asked Versace, somewhat unnerved because he had been given just one week to think about the matter. According to Maria Luisa

Agnese, writing in *Panorama*, Versace replied, "Because we want the best." And, added the journalist, "who better than Calabrese, who not long ago supplied Fiat with three hundred names for cars and trucks, among them the winning Ritmo, Panda and Prisma?" (all names of Fiat and Lancia models). The clever "blady" wouldn't last long as a name, however, because Versace's creative turnover was so fevered that his styles never settled into a definitive mold. In this same collection he presented his first targeted prints, in which the design was stamped on the cloth at particular points linked to the layout of the paper pattern. It was a technique Versace would use again and again until it became one of his signatures.

Economically speaking, it was a magic moment for Versace. But at just that moment, when Italian design was at its peak of consumer desirability all around the world, signs of trouble were brewing. The turning point came on October 19, 1987, when the New York Stock Exchange, in what became known as Black Monday, lost more than 500 points on the Dow Jones index. In a single day, $750 billion dollars in stocks went down the drain in markets around the world, and America received a brusque wake-up call from the Reagan-era dream that had puffed up the economy like whipped cream. Astronomical fortunes based on junk bonds were swept away, and an entire class and way of life—the yuppie social climbers—were laid low. In the first semester of 1988, total Italian exports of clothing to the U.S. fell by 7 percent. And the trend was destined to get worse. The contraction of the American market would culminate, two years later, in financial crisis and in a few cases, outright bankruptcy for department stores in New York, Dallas and Minneapolis.

In February 1988, Gianni Versace S.p.A. recovered possession of the titles to Gianni Versace perfumes for men and women, buying them from Yves Saint Laurent, which only a year before had acquired them from the cosmetics giant Charles of the Ritz. According to the French, the Versace cosmetics line was then worth 20 billion lire in annual sales. "The purchase of Versace perfumes by Gianni Versace is part of a general trend," wrote leading economic journalist Federico Rampini, then Paris correspondent for *Il Sole 24 Ore*. "In the past decade, many fashion designers began to associate their names with new cosmetic products in order to take advantage of the 'economies of scale' of their brand name value. In those days they couldn't sustain the costs of production, promotion and sales of these perfumes.... But today things have changed and those who have the means are trying to buy back the cosmetics brands that bear their names."

Versace could bring his precious perfumes home because his accounts were thriving. The group's direct and indirect sales (outright sales plus those from products made and sold under the Versace name by other companies) amounted to 390 billion lire, close to that of Armani. For the top two in terms of sales continued to be those old rivals Versace and Armani, with their other competitors somewhere behind: Gianfranco Ferré at 320 billion lire, the Fendi sisters at 250 billion, Missoni at 135 billion. That same month, the shareholding structure of the Gianni Versace group changed. Claudio Luti, one of the two CEOs, decided to leave his position and put his minority share—that is, 20 percent of the holding Versace Finanziaria S.p.A.—up for sale. The Versace brothers had first rights on his share and they exercised that option without even waiting for the expiration date of March 5. Santo Versace decided it was worth shelling out 12.5 billion lire to purchase Luti's share. But they still had to settle the value of Luti's other shares: 10 percent of Gianni Versace S.r.l., 10 percent of GiVi, and 8 percent of Alias, the clothing factory belonging to the group, where some hundred people were employed. In just a few months they came to an agreement to buy these for a total of some 20 billion lire. Now Gianni Versace S.p.A. was entirely in the hands of the three Versace siblings—Gianni, Santo and Donatella—who owned 45, 35 and 20 percent shares respectively. The three were in tune with each other, looking ahead to the future with great enthusiasm. "We need to exploit all our potential," Santo told Alan Friedman of the *Financial Times*. "Gianni is younger than Armani and Valentino and still has a lot of give, but we also hope that Versace will survive and prosper as a company that goes on much longer than Gianni Versace."

Gianni agreed with Santo. "We don't have time for self-congratulation. We Italians cannot stay still. We have the most beautiful fabrics in the world and unlimited talent. Certainly, we can't continue to grow at 30 or 40 percent a year. We now have to accept the fact that our annual sales will grow at 10 or 15 percent. And Europe is becoming a more important market for us than the United

States." Although, Santo was convinced, "there's still room to grow in the U.S. market."

In March that year Versace introduced the Update line, in which his sister Donatella and brother-in-law Paul Beck were design partners. First he showed the menswear, its leading item inspired by Bim, the protagonist of Béjart's *Souvenir de Léningrad*. It was a suit with trousers that were a touch clownish, a pop art shirt and a roomy jacket that looked like something from his grandfather's wardrobe. These styles—the slightly crazy jackets, the trousers that looked like they came from a dancer's closet or from an athlete's locker, the rockers' jewelry—were designed for young men from 15 to 25, and they offered more affordable prices than the Istante line, which had returned to the market in 1985. Three months later, the Update womenswear line came out. This was Gianni Verace's response to the overdose of jeans that had spilled onto the market as second lines from all the big designer labels—lines with names like Emporio Armani, Valentino Jeans, and Oaks by Ferré. "If I had decided to do a jeans line," Versace told Maria Vittoria Carloni in *Panorama*, "I could have counted on 40 billion lire in sales right away, because jeans are a great way to make money. But the very young, in my opinion, don't really identify with the so-called jeans generation."

A few months later Versace would be awarded the U.S. fashion prize Cutty Sark, the only American prize for menswear, handed out yearly to the best designer internationally by a panel of U.S. journalists. It was the second time Versace had won the prize; he had received his first Cutty Sark in 1983. The jury praised Versace for the unusual technical and creative answers he gave to design problems. And not long afterward, America would also confer on Versace the prestigious Stanley Award, a sort of Oscar for lifetime achievement that the designer traveled to Dallas to receive.

As the year neared its close, Versace triumphed on the runways of Milan, earning the praise of fashion critic Suzy Menkes, who had just taken over the job at the *International Herald Tribune*. "Versace's daytime look was a jacket, waist- or hip-length but always molded to the body and teamed with pants that looked fresh and sporty.... The new pant has flat pleats in front, is plain in the back, and falls gently to the ankles. It is sure to be copied as much as Versace's 'millefeuille' skirt that is selling everywhere." For evening, Versace matched pants and bustiers highly decorated with embroidery and appliques. It was just a hint of what the fashion world would be seeing soon, when Versace sent out his couture fashion, Atelier Versace, in Paris. Yes, he had decided to launch himself into yet another new adventure: making one-off, exclusive clothes for clients who were equally exclusive. Exceptional clothes to be designed and sewn in the atelier that Gianni had built into his headquarters at Via Gesù—a workshop with twenty-four dressmakers, a reception room for clients and another room to showcase his designs. It was a sort of sentimental return to his origins, to his mother's dressmaking shop where Gianni had imbibed fashion from his very childhood. And in fact there was a black-and-white photo of his mother alongside the photos of supermodels and futuristic clothes that Mimmo Rotella had fashioned into a brightly colored collage to decorate the walls of the atelier.

But it was above all the success of the limited Couture line that he had introduced alongside his ready-to-wear fashion two years before, that convinced Versace that the time had come to devote himself to a more personalized, elite kind of fashion. After all, who better than Versace, a grand couturier on the level of a Dior, a Saint Laurent, to aspire to create high fashion? But what gave his creations a different flavor was the spark he got from the theater. "The idea of Atelier comes out of a need for freedom," Gianni Versace told *L'Espresso*. "It's the desire to gamble, to enjoy myself, the way I do when I create costumes for the theater. I imagine this atelier of mine as something like an old-fashioned artist's workshop, where creativity can be expressed freely, and widely. A workshop of ideas, a place that's also open to technical discovery and other kinds of experimentation. My costumes for the theater will also be born here, and I hope that will bring about a process of osmosis between clothing for the stage and clothing for life."

That kind of transfer of ideas between ballet costumes and Versace's fashion collections had always been there, right from the designer's first activities for the theater. And now, big international celebrities were giving a shine to his stage-worthy clothes. For Sting, Versace designed a tailcoat that transformed into a dinner jacket, eliminating the need to change costumes during the performance. Jane Fonda ordered twelve outfits plus accessories from Atelier; Faye Dunaway ordered three, Cher took two—and Elton John, fifteen. These were clothes that cost from 3 to 20 million lire apiece. Clothes that enthralled the high-toned crowd at the gala evening at Paris's Musée d'Orsay on January 25, 1989: three hundred invited guests including the godmother of the occasion, Danielle Mitterand; Culture Minister Jack Lang and his wife, writer Françoise Sagan; and the Italian ambassador, Serena Attolico. They watched the presentation of Versace's clothes and the film that documented his artistic relationship with Béjart, *La fortuna dell'amicizia* directed by Sergio Salerni based on an idea by Anna Piaggi.

His escort and guide in this society preview, as in a second presentation in July at the Musée Jacquemart-André, was his friend Wanda Galtrucco, who remembers fondly the day Gianni asked her to help. "I was on the *dormeuse* in the sitting room watching the news on TV. Gianni called me. I said, 'Do you want to go to a film this evening?' He said: 'My brother and sister and I think it's time I moved into high fashion. It's such a showcase, it makes such an important statement. Would you like to help out?' I told him I had never had a job. He said, 'If I wanted a professional, I could hire anybody I wanted. But I need you, because you also know how to look after the social side of things.' So I discussed it with my husband and my children, and they told me it was a marvelous idea. But I was afraid, afraid this might ruin my friendship with Gianni. He, however, reassured me: 'We'll always remain friends. And if there's anything wrong, we'll talk about it.'

Gianni was always very frank and so was I. I said yes, and I was there right until the end."

In April, Versace's clothes were once again on show in a museum. This time they were showcased in the most beautiful exhibit ever dedicated to the designer, called *Gianni Versace, l'abito per pensare* (*Gianni Versace, Fashion for Thought*) and mounted by the city of Milan under Mayor Paolo Pillitteri in the ballroom of the Castello Sforzesco. Two hundred items plus fifteen theatrical costumes explained who Gianni Versace was and how he had gotten where he was in just ten years. Guido Vergani, writing in *la Repubblica*, summed up the exhibit well. "The title of the show," wrote Vergani, "might sound a bit foolish because it seems to suggest something paradoxical, the kind of clever comment a designer might toss off and which the press and the arts world would then dutifully take seriously because of the great influence that fashion world people exert. But even a quick visit to the show in Milan will convince you that the title is not intellectual sham." Because not only were the clothes beautiful and the design of the exhibit effective, "but even the most distracted of visitors will note, on the walls beside or behind the clothes, notes, dates, photographs, captions. And he or she will understand that the designer's trench coat, his leotard, fabrics and accessories have all been thought out very carefully. It's something very new, and not just for Italy. Even at the celebrated show of works by Yves Saint Laurent curated by Diana Vreeland for the Metropolitan Museum of Art in New York, there was nothing more than a series of beautiful dresses, chosen with intelligence and presented with great style."

In Milan, however, there was more. "The exhibit dedicated to Gianni Versace," Vergani continued, "aims not only to document the creative itinerary of an international designer, it aims to analyze it, just as would be done in a serious retrospective of any figurative artist." The curators of the exhibit, fashion historian Nicoletta Bocca and fabric expert Chiara Buss, had done something new: "They have studied Gianni Versace's work methods carefully in order to invent a grammar for fashion, allowing them to discuss the clothes impartially."

It had taken more than a year of work to prepare, hard work because it involved creating an interaction between the designer and his assistants, on the one hand, and on the other, the committee of experts that included museum directors like Alessandra Mottola Molfino and Cristina Piacenti, and academics like Grazietta Butazzi and Omar Calabrese. "I had no idea what was going on, I was completely out of it," a cheerful Versace told Vergani. "The important thing, however, is that these women, who were so punctilious—even so boring sometimes—got me to understand a whole bunch of things about myself and about my work!" At the last moment, Versace changed some of the clothes on exhibit. And Gianfranco Cavaglià, the architect responsible for mounting the show, admitted, "he was right, because clothes are different from all other objects made by man and they need to be matched with their surroundings in a very particular way." Everyone who saw the exhibit (and that includes this writer) can still summon up the glimmer of the chain mail, the lushness of some of the evening dresses, the graphic silhouettes of some pairs of jackets and skirts—the whole vision of Versace's oeuvre, so astounding and rich, so monumental.

It was a perfect moment for Versace. Both his shows of 1989, the one in March presenting the fall-winter 1989–1990 collection and the one in October presenting the spring-summer 1990 collection, got raves from the Italian and international press. In March, Versace was already drawing attention. Were other designers showing a chaste, simple, pared-down model of femininity? Well, he would go against the grain, as always. Natalia Aspesi, reporting in *la Repubblica*, summed it up: "Gianni Versace's show at Milano Collezioni at the Fair is one constant hum of whispers and excitement, building up to a liberatory ovation. With reckless daring, the Calabrian designer has defeated the Khomeinist fashion trend, which would like to bury women and make them luxuriously invisible…. He has thrown all caution to the wind, giving women back that seductive violence that may one day soon be declared blasphemous…. Against the grain of the many designers who sent out unattractive models on their runways, he chose only models of stunning—and for ordinary women mortifying—beauty, and he showed them off in skirts that not only ended just a few inches below the bikini line, but also wrapped around sarong-style, so that at every step that hypnotic triangle of bare skin would open up to the point where the modesty-minded could only be advised to keep their eyes shut."

The show gathered speed. "And then comes a charge, an insurrection," Aspesi continued, "a hands-on battle of short black sheaths of wool and velvet, as serviceable as bank accounts; of perfect long jackets tailored in menswear fabrics over black velvet miniskirts; of pernicious *plissé* sunbursts that can transform any part of the body into a target; of black velvet pants that do nothing to hide the legs because there's a naughty slit on one side that runs up to the waist; of evening dresses with tiny, scandalously lavish bodices and transparent wrapped skirts of ruffled chiffon; of long gowns, practically crinolines, made of gauze completely covered with embroidery patterns somewhere between Depero and the Russian avant-garde—clothes that cost 40 million lire and up and that every billionaire who's still in his right mind should buy for his *signora*, as long as she's beautiful. In any case, they only cost half of what a Mercedes goes for."

Suzy Menkes of the *International Herald Tribune* agreed, leading off enthusiastically: "Versace's show was so confident in his sensual message, his models so joyous in their leg show, that you had to wonder whether Versace isn't right, and the other designers in Milan wrong as they opt for longer, sober hemlines."

There was more praise to come for Versace in October, when he presented the spring-summer 1990 fashions. There were suits with very short skirts in loud colors of yellow, orange and green; dresses in shiny, opaque satin; tiny tops and bras in gold and jewels worn with simple silk wrap skirts. The pinnacle of luxury and sex appeal.

CHAPTER 11
The Glamour Man

At the turn of the 1990s, high fashion, luxury Italian prêt-à-porter reached its zenith. Italian style had taken the trophy in Paris, where the French could boast Lagerfeld, Jean-Paul Gaultier and the Japanese, but not a solid industrial base behind their fashion. Meanwhile Italian fashion rested on a firm entrepreneurial footing—companies making thread, textiles, clothes and accessories—and a very efficient system connecting business, image and communication in the city of Milan. The fashion designers, who were the engine of this kind of development (which also took off in Japan beginning in 1989), were now working to give a distinctive definition to their style. And this was what Gianni Versace was trying to do as he "heightened" his style in the much-applauded collections of the period. Writing in *Il Messaggero* of Versace's spring-summer 1990 collection, Pia Soli said he was "that combative designer who pursues his own course with the usual violence and with an expansive curiosity that all give him credit for." Versace left no one unmoved. "Just a few words are needed to define his collection, which measures about 10 billion lire by some fifty-eight minutes: color, embroidery, gold, embroidery, fringe, embroidery, *nappa*, embroidery, and then short, sexy, clingy, provocative, fun, sarong, jumpsuits, shawls, toreador, heels, chains, *bijoux*, pants, top—all for a woman half-Jane, half-Nefertiti; half-Cleopatra, half-empress Theodora; half-Jessica, half-empress Messalina." It was the very essence of Versace's work, that collection, what semiotician Omar Calabrese calls his "neo-Baroque" style in his essay in the catalogue *L'abito per pensare*. "The neo-Baroque is an overall formal approach that we find in all Versace's work, even when his influences seem to come from an updated classicism, or from romantic tendencies, or even from the reworking of the historic avant-gardes of the early 20th century. It's an approach that can be seen not only in the designer's actual tailored garments but even more in the way he displays them and narrates them, that is, in his communicative style—which emerges from the photographs, from his advertising campaigns, and from all the collateral activities that surround the presentation of the collection and the accessories."

Where do we see this neo-Baroque in Versace? First of all, in the designer's appetite for the theatrical, for the mise en scène, both in his clothes, which aimed to be a little bit exhibitionist, and in the way they were presented in ad campaigns by great photographers from Avedon to Newton, telling stories in which "every picture is the movie still of a performance." And of course Versace's love of the mise en scène was also apparent in his passion for designing costumes for the stage. There was a craving for excess in all of this, Calabrese observes "scenic excess, as when he pushes the boundaries of exoticism in the way he presents things, in the jumble of quotations from antiquity, in the revival of a rich, decadent style (drawing on everything from Delacroix to D'Annunzio, from Italian Mannerism to the thirties)." And there was an expressive excess, in the detail of the clothes and in their asymmetry. There was a "constant ludic atmosphere, in which every gesture marks a desire to express oneself at the very limit of the acceptable, of normality, taking care however not to cross the line that would lead straight to bad taste if poorly played out."

There was no place for normality in Gianni Versace's esthetic, even though the normal must surely have marked a part of his daily life: the meetings with his colleagues, the family Christmases, the intimate moments with Antonio, the cakes his cooks Alba and Lucia baked, the movies with friends. The moments that granted him the emotional balance he needed to concentrate, to create. And which demonstrated that his large horizons, his tendency—in his fashion, his homes, in the people he liked to frequent—to be a little bit over the top, were part of a huge desire to affirm himself. Beginning with his amazing clothes, so sexy and so impeccably constructed, so new and stunning season after season, Versace built a golden, protected world around himself in which he was the absolute sovereign. It was a universe of *glamour*, that is, of enchantment, magic, fascination. It was there that Versace liked to be and there that he wanted to take those who bought his clothes and even those who just came close to have a look, to catch a whiff of the scent.

In the last years of the 1980s, Versace had yet another brainstorm. He had always adored beautiful women, right from the beginning of his ad campaigns with Avedon. But now he wanted even more. "I remember the moment well," says David Brown, then the director of one of the most important modeling agencies, Riccardo Gay. "That was the time when the mannequins, alluring women who knew how to wear clothes on the runway like Dalma, Amalia and Pat Cleveland—were replaced by the supermodels. It was Gianni who started it. He wanted to see the cover girls of the moment on his runway, the magazine stars. It was a logical thing for someone like him, who always wanted the best of the best, but it changed the fashion shows. Because the models who appeared on the covers of *Vogue, Harper's Bazaar* and *W* had names like Cindy Crawford and Linda Evangelista. And soon there would be Versace's famous trio— Evangelista, Naomi Campbell and Christy Turlington. At first it wasn't even so much a question of fees: a model might be paid a million, or a million and a half lire [approximately $1,000] to take part in a show. The problem was to convince the models, who worked out of New York for the great international fashion magazines and for the ad campaigns of American designers, to come to Milan. And then one of them began to ask for more money and the prices began to skyrocket, and soon all of them were asking $5,000 or $10,000 a show. And the prices would go up even more in the following years—to $15,000, $20,000. In those days, to model for Gianni Versace meant you had arrived."

Following the first supermodels came others—Stephanie Seymour, Claudia Schiffer, Karen Mulder, Yasmeen Ghauri, Helena Christensen, Carla Bruni, Eva Herzigova, Kate Moss. Names that at the end of the eighties and through the nineties represented the ideal of beauty of the globalized world—the role the movie stars of Hollywood once played in the collective imagination. "But it was Gianni who got it all started," says Brown. "Gianni left all the business of the contracts and the dates in the hands of his trusted fashion coordinator Angelo Azzena, but from the human point of view, he maintained a direct contact with his models. Naomi, who was his muse for so many years, always referred to him as someone who believed in her and who would give her advice as if he were a father, a brother, a friend. Gianni also had a special relationship with Linda Evangelista, while Christy Turlington withdrew from his shows fairly soon, in part because for a long time she had an exclusive, 24-carat gold contract with Ralph Lauren. Each of them, however, wanted to be Gianni's favorite, and he was marvelous at treating them all in the same way."

The supermodels made Gianni Versace's fashion shows a fashion week must. People practically came to blows with each other to get a seat. Natalia Aspesi recalls the opening of the fall-winter 1989 collection show in March 1989, when Versace staged a sort of tableau vivant in which the James Bond film actress Talisa Soto, Cindy Crawford and the gorgeous Somali princess Iman were wearing "magnificent dressing gowns of silk velvet that slip down their shoulders and part over their legs, revealing opulent bloomers. Languorous and indolent, they stretch, make up their faces and study themselves in the mirror." The following season, Iman would have an exclusive deal with Versace. As he explained, "This year, too, I have chosen beautiful models, because beauty is indispensible in a fashion show. Beauty heightens fashion; it makes fashion into legend. And also, the women of today, even those who will never get up on a runway, want the product, which is going to be ready for them to buy in a few months, to be as desirable as possible." As if his breathtaking shows had any need of explanation.

"Versace is one of the biggest leaders in the fashion world," Liz Tilberis, then editor in chief of *Harper's Bazaar*, said at the time. "His mark is unmistakable, courageous, bold, sexy and always sumptuous. And his presentation is exceptional: Versace's show is one of the high points of the fashion calendar." Anna Wintour of *Vogue* America put it this way: "Gianni Versace is not afraid to dazzle. He dazzled us with colors, styles, ornament and leather in ready-to-wear collections that are always just about to go over the top. He also dazzled us with his ability to entertain the public, with his superstar models on the runways and in his highly inventive advertising campaigns." Ingrid Sischy, in *Interview*, wrote: "A show by Gianni Versace wakes you up. It's fast, it leaves you with your mouth open, it makes you laugh and it gives you the idea that anything is possible."

Gianni Versace's runway shows also relied on another powerful ingredient—music. Gianni had always loved rock music, right back to the days of Studio 54 in New

York; it inspired his first collections in the 1970s. In an article published in 1989 in *Il Messaggero*, Versace wrote: "At the first rock concert I ever attended, years ago in Paris, I found myself standing on a chair howling—I who usually act pretty calm and collected. My clothes, it seems, transmit something that rock people are able to perceive better than anyone else. Perhaps they feel the clothes are in sync with their musical expression—that's something I find very stimulating." Certainly, rock stars went crazy for Versace's clothes. Elton John, every time he went shopping, bought dozens of versions of a single classic style in different colors, then laid on accessories and jewelry and his own extravagant hats. Sting was also a fan; he might put on a dark violet coat over a nude torso with a pair of tuxedo trousers underneath.

And then there were Bruce Springsteen, Prince, Tina Turner (who loved his leather styles), Michael Jackson, even Paul McCartney, who told Versace he'd like to keep the clothes the designer had made for the videoclip of *Say Say Say*, and thereafter became his loyal client. Eric Clapton always bought up most of Versace's menswear collection, until, after the death of his young son Conor, he switched to the more discreet style of Giorgio Armani. And Versace really loved their music. It gave him a charge, and he often listened to it while he worked. "I love to be in touch with rockers because they have the energy of our times, a contagious, positive energy. I'm certain that a fashion designer's creativity can benefit enormously from the electrifying music of a Springsteen or the tender, sophisticated intelligence of a Sting." The rock stars felt

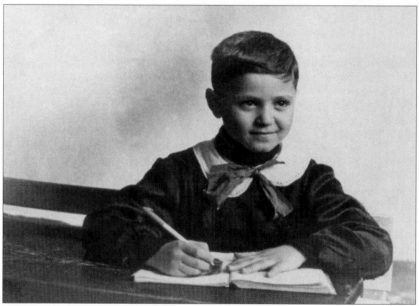

Top left: Gianni, Donatella and Santo Versace at the beach in Reggio Calabria.
Top right: Gianni with sister Donatella, celebrating her second birthday.
Bottom: Gianni Versace at school. © Anchor GBB/Grazia Neri

Franca, Gianni's mother.

Top: Antonio, his father.
Bottom: Family portrait with Gianni's parents in front of the Reggio Calabria house, 1976.

Santo and Donatella Versace with brother Gianni, 1997. © Olycom

Gianni Versace, portrait by Mark Harbeit.

Gianni Versace with his niece Allegra and his nephew Daniel, the children of his sister Donatella and Paul Beck, Villa Fontanelle, 1992.

On Lake Como with Allegra, 1993. © G. Giansanti/Grazia Neri

Top: Gianni Versace and Antonio D'Amico in the desert, Sudan, 1989.
Bottom: At Key West, 1995.

Gianni Versace and Antonio D'Amico, portrait by Herb Ritts.

Top: Gianni Versace with Elton John at St. Tropez, 1992.
Bottom: With Gigi Scagliotti in the desert, Algeria, 1998.

Gianni Versace and Richard Avedon at the inauguration of "Evidence 1944–1994,"
a retrospective of the photographer's work at Palazzo Reale, Milan, 1995.
© Roxanne Lowit

Gianni Versace in silhouette against a painting by Mimmo Paladino, 1993.
© Toni Thorimbert/Sygma/Corbis

The stylist at Villa Fontanelle, Moltrasio (Como).

Villa Fontanelle, Moltrasio, on Lake Como. This was Gianni's favorite house.
© Ron Sachs/CNP/Corbis

Interiors of Villa Fontanelle. © Ron Sachs/CNP/Corbis

Casa Casuarina, Gianni Versace's residence in Miami. © Massimo Listri/Corbis

Top: Pool with mosaic based on favorite Versace motifs.
Bottom: Dining room decorated with Home Collection. © Massimo Listri/Corbis

Top: October 1991, Milan. Gianni Versace with his models at the spring-summer 1992 show. © Vittoriano Rastelli/Corbis
Bottom: July 1996, Paris. Versace with supermodels Linda Evangelista, Kate Moss and Naomi Campbell following the Atelier collection fall-winter 1996–1997 show. © B.D.V./Corbis

Actress Elizabeth Hurley at the première of the film *Four Weddings and a Funeral* in a punk-style gown by Versace created for spring-summer 1994.
© LFI Masterphoto

Asymmetric jacket from the fall-winter 1998–1999 collection. © FIRSTVIEW.COM

Versace's Baroque, fall-winter 1991–1992 collection. © FIRSTVIEW.COM

Carla Bruni in crinoline matched with jeans shirt, from the Signature collection, spring-summer 1992. © FIRSTVIEW.COM

Naomi Campbell wearing S&M dress from the fall-winter 1992–1993 collection.

Claudia Schiffer in a Versace suit, the cover of *Time*, April 17, 1995.

With choreographer Maurice Béjart.
Sketch for costume of the Béjart ballet *Dionysus*, 1987.

Dress inspired by the works of artist Sonia Delaunay, fall-winter 1989–1990 collection.
© Olycom

Eleven-colored print based on Andy Warhol portraits, from the spring-summer 1991 collection. © Olycom

Both patterns (across and above) were exhibited at the Victoria and Albert Museum in London for the 2002 retrospective dedicated to Versace.

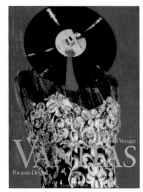

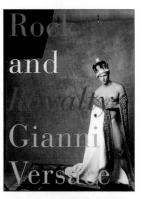

Covers of Gianni Versace's books: the many facets of a glamorous world.

the same sympathy for Versace and after a concert, they were happy to spend a few days on Lake Como at Villa Fontanelle, where Versace received them with all the munificence of a prince. "In the four days that Springsteen was a guest at my house," Versace told the news magazine *Panorama*, "I was quite amazed by how natural he was, his great simplicity and freshness. Only when I went to his concert did I understand what a legend he is, the unexpected force he emanates, a force that moves everyone and draws all 70,000 young people present into one great musical mania."

As for Sting, Versace said, "some of his songs are extraordinary. 'Desaparecidos' is one of the greats of the last few years, along with 'Fragile.' The latter, which talks about our fragility in the world today, to me is one of the most disturbing reflections on all that is happening around us." His relationship with Prince was not as close, given the singer's eccentricities. Versace recalled that "Prince was the guest of my sister and brother-in-law on Lake Como. I didn't see much of him. I was quite shocked to find that it was only after three days that he learned the house was on the lake, because he spends all his time in the dark. I like his music a lot and I think he has a lot of magnetism on the stage, something you don't feel when you meet him in person. But his music, like that of other great rock stars, accompanies all of the changes our generation goes through."

He liked rock, but not only. As he did with his clothes, Versace liked to mix different styles of music. While he was getting ready to assemble what would be the soundtrack for his fashion show, for weeks he would listen to cuts from all the hot artists of the moment, prepared for him by Angelo Azzena. He picked the ones that really gave him a charge. Then he mixed them with other music, which he listened to at various times throughout his long work days, often in the car between Milan and the villa on Lake Como. The music was also one of the reasons why a show by Versace was always an amazing display of fireworks. The classiest models of the day moved down the runway to the beat of Elton John's "Sacrifice," or Italian balladeer Fabrizio de André's "Creuza de mä" in Ligurian dialect, or "Nessun dorma" sung by Luciano Pavarotti—Versace the first to use the aria on the fashion runway. But the models also kept time to Gregorian chant, perhaps mixed with down-to-earth Calabrian regional songs and the folk harmonies of Hugues Le Bars, a composer Versace discovered through Maurice Béjart and his ballets. The music gave Versace's fashion shows an extra edge.

"Gianni was an extraordinary communicator," says Emanuela Schmeidler, who was Versace's chief press officer for fifteen years, until 1999. "He knew, better than anyone else, how to impart—with his clothes, his shows, his advertising campaigns, the media coverage of his houses, the CDs, the ballets, the art exhibits and the books—his dream of glamour and, finally, a certain style of life. And this is a strategy that is still being used by Versace today." Richard Martin, writing in the introduction to the catalogue for the exhibition *Gianni Versace* at the Fondazione Ratti, says, "Of central importance in Versace's work is his cleverness in interpreting fashion as an art made for the media. Not only does he throw his work into the ravishing jaws of the contemporary celebrity media with his runway shows and his connections with rock music, ballet and theater, but he appropriates the charisma of media people, working in complete harmony with them. His clothes beam out all their power under the lights of the movie camera, the runway spots, and the revealing eye of the videocam. Versace designed for a generation that was hungry for visibility and saturated by the media, people who became adults in the last quarter of the 20th century. When it comes to contemporary fashion and especially to Versace, the cynics say, take away the rock and roll, the advertising money and the supermodels, and what's left? The answer, they think, is going to be: nothing.

"But for Versace, the answer is that he continues to create incredible clothes that still reflect the indomitable spirit of the late 20th century."

CHAPTER 12

Paris, New York

"Breathless" pretty well sums up how 1990 began for Gianni Versace. He had just finished baptizing the new line Versus, aimed at young people and designed by his sister Donatella. He celebrated the line at the end of 1989 at the Superstudio in Milan, at a party characterized by pounding rock music, rivers of champagne and throngs of models wandering among the guests. He was already working on another one of his little coups. In mid-January at Milan's menswear shows, he introduced his tie-free male. Eric Clapton, in town for a rare testimonial, kicked off his world tour the same night as Versace's runway presentation "wearing an outfit that spells out Versace's esthetic philosophy—a black blazer as soft as a sweater and black trousers without a hint of a crease," Laura Asnaghi wrote in *la Repubblica*. Versace also designed Clapton's guitars and guitar strap, decorated with Futurist designs and glittering with colored beads.

For fall-winter 1990–1991, Versace showed clothes that were decidedly un-classic—sweaters worn over bare skin, skin-tight leather trousers, shirts wide open over the chest, a lot of black and a lot of color. "Versace is the Barnum of Italian fashion," wrote John Fairchild, the powerful publisher of *Women's World Daily*. Versace laughed at that definition: "I'm pleased to be compared to Barnum. With all the boring ideas going around, someone has to break the rules." And break them he did. Arguing, for example, that "the necktie no longer stands for respectability, because today even criminals wear them." The next day that quip grabbed all the headlines, for he always knew how to wow the media. He even earned the animosity of the tie makers, who published a full-page advertisement in the papers offering apologies to all the respectable men who had been insulted by Versace's remarks. At this point Versace called his lawyers to ask for damages and the dispute went on for a while. In the end, the jury for advertising ethics ruled that Versace's decision to ban neckties from his upcoming menswear collections should not be construed as denigrating the necktie and those who made it—it was just a provocation. As it happened, Versace's provocation went far beyond the tie to cover an entire institution, for in the years to come the stuffy bourgeois suit inspired by English bespoke tailoring would lose more and more of its appeal. A new style of dress for men would catch on, even in office wear—a more informal look that would culminate in the custom of "Friday fashion," as the business world abandoned jacket and tie on Friday in preparation for the weekend.

Versace actually published a book on the matter, titled *L'uomo senza cravatta* (*Men Without Ties*), where in addition to spelling out his vision of male style, he homed in on the kind of masculine body he preferred: broad shoulders, narrow waist and muscled legs. As Richard

Martin wrote in that book, "With reference to the body shape that Versace prefers, the necktie is superfluous, if not actually visually noxious, for the very presence of a tie would diminish the extreme triangulation of the torso. The tie, which so obviously connects the torso to the waist, can only limit Versace's pleasure in narrowing the waist and conceiving the masculine body as an aggregate of perfect forms." Versace, he wrote, would like to "break the mold of the bourgeois male to explore the potential of a man who is sensual, projecting a strong sense of male identity mixed with iconic style." It was very much what Versace tried to do with women's fashion—constantly seeking to emphasize the shape of the female body. But apparently, playing with male stereotypes was much more transgressive.

Just a few days later, on January 20, Versace was poised for the difficult, demanding challenge he had been preparing for a couple of years: haute couture. His Atelier Versace debuted amid the marble and plasterwork of the Ritz in Paris—a hotel that was among other things, Coco Chanel's home for the last years of her life—where he led off the haute couture fashion shows for spring-summer. Following Valentino, who had left Rome to show his haute couture in the City of Light, and Gianfranco Ferré, who was at work there trying to bring back the glory days of Dior, now it was Versace's turn. He had been spending sleepless nights putting the finishing touches on the space where the show would be staged, assisted by director Sergio Salerni and a team so detail-minded they were downright obsessed. And now it was all ready. Karl

Lagerfeld, whom Gianni considered a sort of legend and who was a dear friend, sent him a little sketch—a profile of Gianni with an affectionate message. He would provide one of those messages each time Gianni sent out a show in Paris, always with a touch of irony, as when he depicted Gianni in the toga of a Roman emperor.

Three hundred guests were in the audience for the biggest novelty of the Paris season. Julie Andrews sat in the front row in a black Versace suit (Versace designed her costumes and those of Marcello Mastroianni for the film *Cin Cin*). Jacqueline Bisset was also in the front row, and then there were all the stylish ladies of Paris and Milan, and the influential journalists from America, and scores of taste-makers from the art and performance worlds. Versace had already promised Paola Pisa of *Il Messaggero* that "there's no way clients will find bows or ruches or any of the rest of that sort of fussy stuff with me. I have tried to combine high fashion, something I have always loved and that I watched my mother create, with the avant garde, with my passion for modernity. And so I'm appealing to a young, hip woman who wants an exclusive item of clothing but who also wants it to be dynamic."

Down the runway came tops glittering with gemstones paired with super-short skirts or satin shorts, pinstripe suits over beaded bra-tops, little black sheaths so short they approached the limits of obscene but which were lit up with buttons as gorgeous as jewels, a profusion of silks printed in brilliant, aggressive, shocking patterns and colors. For evening, as the speakers played Pavarotti singing "Nessun dorma" and the triumphant finale

"Vincerò" rang out, Versace offered short dresses of tulle and jet with transparent and embroidered shawls bearing love notes to Paris in the form of quotations from modernist artists like Robert and Sonia Delaunay, Raoul Dufy and Kees Van Dongen. This was Versace's homage to the French capital's eternal spirit of the avant- garde. Versace's suits cost from some $7,500 to $15,000; his cocktail dresses from $18,000 to $60,000; his evening dresses $90,000. These were clothes for ladies of the jet set, but above all for the Hollywood stars who were Versace's clients—Barbra Streisand, Joan Collins, Jane Fonda, etc.

The look for fall-winter 1990–1991, which debuted in March, would be short, short, short. All the designers—all of them, including Armani—took a pair of scissors to their hemlines, as Versace had done the previous season. Natalia Aspesi, writing in *la Repubblica*, spoke of a "Faustian" revolution: "Age may soon be a concept that is pertinent only in round table discussions and for social services that deal with the elderly, a concept that will be utterly banished from the feminine wardrobe. There will no longer be girls, young women, mature women, old ladies—no, fashion will have them all rolled together into an adolescent." Versace sent out tiny dresses that couldn't be shorter, not form-fitting but A-line, worn with transparent stockings rather than the opaque legwear other designers were showing. A fuss arose over Naomi Campbell, whose minuscule thong the audience saw at runway-side. Versace told the press he was proud to have taken a risk with the collection, that he wanted to uncouple women forever from their imitation of men, in clothes and in life. It was as if he was saying, hey, forget about the career woman—who not by chance had always been the fashion symbol of his eternal rival Giorgio Armani.

The Americans liked what Versace was up to. Suzy Menkes, writing in the *International Herald Tribune*, reported the reactions of some U.S. buyers. Andy Basile, Bergdorf Goodman's fashion director, called Versace's clothes "hot enough to burn the hangers in the store." Joan Kaner, fashion director at Neiman Marcus said, "this is Versace at the top of his game. He's kept the sexiness but he's cleaned it up and given it refinement, elegance and that *je ne sais quoi*."

Fashion continued to sparkle, and there were those who would do anything to get an invitation to the post-show party. Versace organized a gala evening for the artist Sebastian Matta and his wife, Germana. He adored art, and this was a clever way to show it.

It was a year of big projects. The first ones involved America, a market that appreciated things by Gianni Versace. With his 120 boutiques strategically placed around the world to back him up, Versace was ready to satisfy his biggest desire. He opened a huge boutique at 817–819 Madison Avenue between the store belonging to Valentino and the one belonging to Armani. The three of them now made up an entire block of Italian style between 68th Street and 69th. The new shop, his second in Manhattan and his biggest store of the eleven Versace boutiques in America, was a 500-square meter building on two floors, with a facade of glass and metal decorated with Corinthian columns. The first floor was devoted to ready-to-wear; the second floor housed his Atelier high-fashion collection. The building was rehabbed by Rocco Magnoli and Lorenzo Carmellini, the veteran designers of his brand who reflected Versace's inimitable style. "I want to present my high-fashion collection directly to elegant American women," Versace told Laura Dubini of the *Corriere della Sera*. "This exclusive type of service is important to me. And I'm also convinced it's important to be present on the American market with my own retail structure. The great, legendary department stores like Saks and Bloomingdale's that introduced Italian fashion to America, are themselves on the market today."

The launch on April 24 was a red carpet show of Manhattan celebrities, among them Robert Wilson, Candice Bergen, and Versace's photographers Richard Avedon, Irving Penn and Bruce Weber, plus show business people like Kim Basinger, Elton John, Jane Fonda, Barbra Streisand, Tina Turner, Eric Clapton and Sting. Tina Brown, the celebrity-tuned editor in chief of *Vanity Fair*, was on hand to give the event her imprimatur. For the opening, Versace prepared a retrospective of forty of his costumes for the ballet and theater.

In June, the costume retrospective moved to Los Angeles where Versace was opening a large new store in Beverly Hills. There was more to Versace's American campaign, however. A few months later he introduced another line, the V2, a menswear line labeled Versace and produced by Zegna, the designer's longtime masculine ready-to-wear and couture manufacturer. V2 aimed to cover the mid-to-high end of the market, slightly below the top line with its clothes that cost $1,400 but well above mass-produced mid-priced clothing. To produce the V2 line, Zegna and Versace created a new company in America, owned 50-50. The wholesale showroom at 745 Fifth Avenue sold the V2 line to retailers from the ground floor and Zegna collections from the second floor. Versace's second menswear line was part of a strategy of broadening the group's product range, which by now ran from high fashion to ready-to-wear, from accessories to watches and perfumes. "Our objective for the nineties," company chairman and CEO Santo Versace told Antonio Calabrò of *la Repubblica*, "is to be present in every luxury goods sector and cover all the market segments for quality clothing." It was a goal Gianni Versace S.p.A. could aim for because its accounts were in excellent shape. "Our sales show constant growth," the chairman and CEO continued. "For 1990, we expect to have more than 220 billion lire in direct sales and 600 billion in indirect sales. And over the next five years, we believe our sales will rise to 400 billion lire, with indirect sales of up to a trillion lire." A rosy forecast that Santo made sure to credit to the talent of his brother, writing in the supplement *Mondo economico* that "the real glue that holds our organization together is Gianni Versace's creativity. As a designer, my brother has always worked at a frenetic, unstoppable pace, and that's the basis of our business plan. Because of our position, and our sales that have never ceased to grow, and which in 1989 grew even more than expected, the company is prepared to face the 1990s in a condition of full financial autonomy."

Their strength was such that Versace could now renegotiate agreements made a decade earlier with partners in Japan, where the company by now controlled twenty-five boutiques, had commercial space in various department stores and sold its products in many multi-brand designer shops. Their objective was to control some ninety shops in Japan by 1992, meanwhile beefing up their presence in department stores.

The group also signed an important new agreement at home. Ittierre, owned by Tonino Perna, which produced the Versus line for Versace, would now be making Versace jeans under a joint venture that would invest 7 billion lire in the Isernia factory to modernize its technological capacities. Versace's Jean Couture (to be produced under different labels for men and women) would be made in denim and silk, in printed denim, in washed, tinted and double-tinted fabrics—the standard five pockets, yes, but very special. The company predicted sales of 400 billion lire for the first five years, of which some 40 percent would be in Italy and the rest abroad. Oh, and Bruce Weber was already in charge of the jeans advertising campaign.

Business was booming and the glamour strategy had taken hold. In June, Versace had another smart idea. He decided he wanted Herb Ritts—the American photographer of the stars, artist of nude studies that had become classics, the most sought-after talent of that moment in fashion photography—to work for him. He wanted four of his supermodels to be photographed together. Ritts shot Naomi Campbell, Christy Turlington, Cindy Crawford and Tatjana Patitz as they nestled up against one another, both sensual and unreachable in their beauty. He placed them in a California desert location, one of those exteriors that he adored and was able to use as if it were a studio, transforming everything in his matchless black and white. Versace shared Ritts's passion for the body, the physical. "I love that reference to sex that's clean, that's natural but powerful," he said. Ritts, for his part, said he hoped "to have succeeded in demonstrating a love for nature and for all that's physical, and to have drawn out of it our present day lifestyle."

Behind this campaign we begin to see for the first time the hand of Donatella Versace, who was already formally in charge of the group's image. Here's how Giusy Ferré of *L'Europeo* reconstructed the story: "It was she who, after the ready-to-wear show in March when Christy Turlington was dressed in the lowest-cut and most-photographed dress of the season, thought of making a bouquet of these four flowers. It was she who played up the malicious, sexy side of the clothes by allowing the girls to choose whatever dress they liked, the dress that made them feel the most spontaneous. With ten years of experience beside photographers and supermodels, Donatella Versace had instinctively picked up on a generational change. 'Christy, Cindy, all of them, they like to dress up, to put on makeup, to wear jewelry. They all have a personal style. Once upon a time the models would show up with their hair a mess, in an old pair of jeans, a big sweater, an ugly old hat. They were trying to hide themselves. Today, however, they are—and they feel themselves to be—onstage.' "

Up until then Donatella had worked behind the scenes, in charge, along with her husband Paul Beck, of shaping the company's image as it connected to rock stars. Elton John, Eric Clapton, Bruce Springsteen, Sting, Prince and Phil Collins were all wearing Versace and all were frequent guests in Milan or at the villa on Lake Como. Now she was 35 years old and wanted her place in the sun. After years of hard, if exciting work backstage with Gianni—and all those conversations with him post–fashion show that went on until four in the morning—after years of exhausting trips to every corner of the globe to follow the group's advertising campaigns, Donatella Versace wanted her share of the limelight. Like the supermodels she loved so dearly. The Italian edition of *Vanity Fair* asked to interview her, with Helmut Newton acting as photographer. Donatella had her picture taken in a form-fitting embroidered jumpsuit along with Paul and their four-year-old daughter Allegra in the lush surroundings of the Jardin Botanique at Cap d'Antibes. Her blonde hair long and straight, "part Brigitte Bardot, part Barbarella, she always wears something tight and black," wrote Glynis Costin in *WWD*. "And she wears a Tiffany diamond and a ruby bracelet that Gianni gave her." About her own appearance, Donatella, who was in her eighth month of pregnancy expecting her second child, told the *WWD* reporter, "I think it's terrible when women don't bother with how they look during pregnancy. I believe you have to look after yourself much more. I'm still wearing high heels, because I feel good in them. They make me feel tall." Costin went on, "Donatella may be small, but her stature at Versace is growing. She's vice president of the brand, she designs the children's line and the accessories, she supervises all the licensing agreements and consults with her designer brother on every aspect of the ready-to-wear and couture collections."

Gianni, for his part, saw his impetuous sister as one of his ideal women. And more: "I don't do anything without asking her, and she does nothing without asking me. She can destroy a whole collection in five minutes, she can make me feel awful, but she can also help me to put it together again in five minutes and make me smile again. That's what I love about her. Our relationship is profoundly sincere." Thus Gianni gave Donatella his imprimatur in the influential news outlet of *WWD*.

As the year drew to a close, Versace once again enjoyed success when the Richard Strauss opera *Capriccio* debuted at the San Francisco War Memorial Opera House, directed by John Cox. The many costumes Versace designed were inspired by Paris haute couture of the twenties—Vionnet, Poiret, Chanel. The acclaim would be matched by that for the Béjart ballet *Pyramide* which went onstage in Cairo, and for which Versace made a vast variety of costumes ranging from ancient Egyptian style to Napoleonic uniforms. And Versace's second show of Atelier fashions at the Ritz in Paris—a profusion of embroidery and prints in which the famous hems had not been lengthened by one inch—was also very well received.

There would also be another novel venture: a new series of books titled *I libri di Versace* that Leonardo Arte, a publisher of coffee table art books under Leonardo Mondadori, devoted to Versace and which were presented at the Frankfurt Book Fair in coeditions with publishers in Europe, the U.S. and Japan. The first volume, titled *I cinque sensi* (*The Five Senses*), was edited by semiotician Omar Calabrese. The second, titled *La mise en scéne*, is dedicated to Maurice Béjart, who also wrote the text. Versace talked about the project proudly, but also with a touch of humility, to Marisa Rusconi of *L'Espresso*. "I've always loved books. My brother Santo passed this enthusiasm along to me. I was just a kid and he would put a copy of Kafka in my hand, and I'd read it and I wouldn't understand anything, and yet, when I was finished there was a great excitement in me. Books are not just made for reading. It's important to look at them and to touch them, too: images have as much to say to me as writing. But maybe this is something I can say because I have never had any pretensions of being an intellectual."

The year 1990 came to a glorious close for Versace. The fashion shows presenting the spring-summer 1991 collections drew their inspiration from the heated, contentious seventies, although none of the designers really wanted to admit it. But especially they promoted the image of a young, fresh and dynamic woman (an image that had been in fashion for a few years now).

Giorgio Armani permitted himself a gibe in the direction of his eternal rival when, interviewed by *Corriere della Sera*, he said he'd be working on "clothes for a woman who's more real, less a fantasy." And that his clothes would be modern, easy to wear, with few trimmings. His jackets, he said, would be long and soft and his skirts above the knee, but the jackets would often be paired with shorts "to show off a woman's legs without putting her panties on display." The allusion to Naomi Campbell's underwear, so visible under her ultra-short skirt to the audience at Versace's last show, could not have been clearer.

Versace, the standard-bearer for short skirts and for fantasy, feared only one thing: becoming a classic. "Nobody blinks an eye anymore if you talk about miniskirts or colors. My attention is now on legs, which I am dressing, binding, painting and tattooing." His spring-summer 1991 collection was in fact a hymn to prints, hyper-colors and embroidery. There were Lycra jumpsuits with Chinese motifs, tiny dresses with designs inspired by Chagall, bodysuits with the face of Marilyn Monroe from Warhol's famous silkscreens (Marilyn turned up again on long evening dresses), stockings and shoes with in-your-face tattoo prints. Suzy Menkes, writing in the *International Herald Tribune*, said that "Versace, who has a house near Como, Italy's silk capital, spent three days a week for seven months working on his sensational prints." She went on to dedicate three-quarters of her report on the fashion shows to Versace. That year he won the Occhio d'Oro prize—awarded by a jury of the international press to the designer who has shown the best work over four seasons—hands down. He dedicated it to fashion designer Enrico Coveri, who had died not long before of a stroke at age 38.

CHAPTER 13

Vulgar? Me?

"In 1991 I'm going to do even more than I did in 1990," Gianni Versace announced as the year began, having just closed the previous incredibly busy twelve months in high style. "My calendar is so full that if I didn't enjoy the work so much, I'd be worried," he told Giusy Ferré of *L'Europeo*. He got a running start. In London, a reception worthy of a king had been prepared for the Calabrian designer. On January 7, the European première of the Strauss opera *Capriccio* directed by John Cox went onstage at the Royal Opera House Covent Garden, following the production's debut in San Francisco in October. On January 8 the exhibit *Versace Teatro* opened at the Henry Moore Gallery of the Royal College of Art, with the participation of Prince Edward, 26. The youngest son of Queen Elizabeth is an art and theater enthusiast who often represents the monarchy on cultural occasions. *Versace Teatro* consisted of 150 costumes that Versace had designed over a decade's work for opera and ballet, from Joseph Russillo's *Lieb und Leid* and Strauss's *Josephs Legende* up to *Capriccio* by way of many ballets for Béjart. But Versace did not just provide the costumes. The designer, with his usual perfectionism, accompanied the costumes for each show with reproductions of the sets, and with drawings, samples of fabrics, embroidery and some items from his fashion collections to show the mutual inspiration between his stage costumes and his fashion design. It was a kind of osmosis that had gratified Versace from the beginning. As he said with enthusiasm, "The theater is a continual source of fresh ideas, a transfusion, an injection of youth for my fashion. A source of knowledge, of maturity."

"I feel more of a painter, an artist studying form, when I work in theater. My model is Léon Bakst," he said of the early 20th-century painter, set designer and costumist for Diaghilev's Ballets Russes. "The costume designer usually adheres to historical reality and rarely expresses his creative freedom. I don't set out to reproduce a period costume. My 18th century, for example, might look like a painting by David Hockney with purple jackets and red T-shirts." The Duchess of Kent nodded; Lord Snowdon, the ex-husband of Princess Margaret smiled; Virgin chief Richard Branson looked curious and Joan Collins pleased for her good friend Gianni, as all sat around the dinner table at the Grosvenor Square residence of Italian ambassador Boris Biancheri. The next morning, Gianni would give a lecture to fashion students at the Royal College of Art, stirring them up with the following words:

"Chic? That's one of the ugliest words in the dictionary. It's used by those who are afraid to be themselves, afraid to dare." When asked the standard question, what's necessary in order to become a designer, Versace replied imperiously: "A very strong ego. Like my own and like that of my sister Donatella." Donatella meanwhile was not in London with her brother, but only because she had just given birth to her second child, Daniel, less than a month previously. But Santo was there, and he lit up with anger when fashion reporters asked him about the slump in the sector. "The big houses will never have a slump," he said. "We're doing extremely well, the store on Via Montenapoleone alone had sales of 14 billion lire this year while the store in New York saw its sales more than double in the past year."

The talk of a downturn in fashion was due to the war. On August 2, 1990, Saddam Hussein invaded Kuwait. And now, on January 17, 1991, the Americans and Europeans agreed to go to war against him. It would be a turning point. A turning point that would also touch the charmed world of fashion, beginning with the haute couture shows in Paris at the end of January. "Passport or invitation in hand, handbags open to be searched, metal-detector wands all over the body," wrote Laura Dubini in *Corriere della Sera.* "The Gulf War and the attack yesterday at the daily *Libération*, the first such attack in Europe since hostilities began, luckily without any victims, have intensified the inspections at the five-day French haute couture shows." In fact, the fashion shows were nearly cancelled. But they took place because from America, three journalists who count announced their arrival: Anna Wintour, editor in chief of *Vogue;* Bernadine Morris, fashion editor of *The New York Times;* and John Fairchild, publisher of *Women's Wear Daily.* But the wealthy American and Arab clients have mostly said no to their invitations, preferring to stay home and watch the videos sent by their favorite couturiers.

Gianni Versace opened the fashion week, offering the following comment on these difficult times: "So there's a war? Saddam Hussein is carrying out ecological terrorism? This, however, is my job. I can't just go and lay off my precious dressmakers. And you know, Atelier is a source of inspiration for all my other collections." This time Versace and his trusted Sergio Salerni, director of his fashion shows in the 1980s and a genius of the necessary technology, wanted something different from the usual, rather traditional reception rooms of the certainly legendary Ritz. Donata Sartorio, then editor of *Lei* and *Per Lui*, recalls the event: "They covered the pool at the Ritz, to which you descended down two stairways from the ground floor, with a huge platform and made the great room into a very welcoming place, very unusual, more suitable for the kind of contemporary luxury that Versace likes to do. I remember a beautiful show, with cleaner lines, more pared-down, as if the purest Versace style had returned, the real couturier look."

There were kimono styles and sack dresses, dresses that bared the arms and plunged in front. To attenuate the shortness of his skirts Versace played around with the hems, which were sometimes rounded, sometimes pointed and sometimes criss-crossed. There was some embroidery, mostly deployed to debunk symbols of power such as sceptres, crowns, coats of arms and even Queen Elizabeth, who was featured on an elegant jacket worn over a pair of jeans.

In February came two important events for Versace: the costumes for a Béjart ballet *La Mort subite,* based on music by Schubert, Kurt Weill and others, sung by Ute Lemper; and a fashion show in Los Angeles on the night of nominations for the Oscars, to raise funds for the fight against AIDS.

When the prêt-à-porter shows came around in March, none of the big fashion houses felt ready to do without the frivolity of seduction and the charm of luxury, no matter how uncertain the times might have been. And least of all Versace. "Anway, in times of crisis," wrote Natalia Aspesi in *la Repubblica*, "nobody's going to kill herself to buy a jacket that's dignified, respectful and high-toned. Glamour alone sells and so next winter we'll see only short skirts, bright colors and prints." The prints that Versace showed for fall-winter 1991–1992 were composed of that Baroque style personally invented by him, made up of bouquets of flowers, greca motifs, scrolls, palmettes and Renaissance patterns in gold and black, which would become his unique signature. "It was a golden color that wasn't flat but was made up of many different tonalities," recalls Patrizia Cucco, Gianni's in-house memory. "I remember that on the blouse worn by Helena Christensen [there's a photo by Herb Ritts in *Versace*, published by Leonardo-De Luca] there were fourteen colors on a single square of print. That print right away became 'Versace's Baroque' in the collective imagination, and it right away became an icon, perhaps even beyond the intentions of Versace himself."

On the runway, however, Versace held back somewhat, showing clothes that hung free of the body, especially from the waist down; new short skirts that were not extremely short—like chiffon kilts or silk skirts with flat pleats worn with black leather jackets—or Empire style and trapeze looks where bodices were revved up with colored satin or gem stones. No sooner had he finished the costumes for his first Shakespeare play, *Richard II* directed by Glauco Mauri, than he found himself the butt of some remarks by his eternal rival Armani, who, perhaps betraying a touch of envy, told the fashion monthly *Moda*, "Let's do away with all those great inventions of yesteryear, those magazine covers showing women who have their backside to the public [the reference is to a cover of *Epoca*, number 2098, dedicated to Versace]. Versace no longer knows how to extricate himself from this print business, because last year everybody told him, 'great, magnificent.'..."

Versace's reply was sharp. "I don't think a beige jacket or a little suit for lesbians is going to be how we remember the nineties. I prefer a woman who's dressed badly but who is free, to an idiot wearing Giorgio Armani." A bit pugnacious himself.

But perhaps he could be forgiven if an authoritative semiotician like Omar Calabrese had decided he merited many pages of fashion analysis in his new book, *Vanitas, lo stile dei sensi* from Leonardo. Calabrese coined the term neo-Baroque to describe Versace's virtuoso technique and the voracious pleasure he took in mixing diverse cultural "quotations" in a highly theatrical performance. With this book—on its cover is a slender Christy Turlington sitting in a lotus position in a gemstone-studded bodice, lush printed pantyhose, and the necklace and bracelets of an

Indian deity—Calabrese puts his definitive spin on the term. And he expands it, writing about the intense physicality of Versace's clothes, which appeal to all the senses: besides vision, they appeal to the sense of touch as they cling to the body, or let it be seen under the flimsiest of fabrics. Music excites the sense of hearing at the runway show, highlighting the various sentiments that inspire the clothes. The particular odors given off by different fabrics stimulate the sense of smell. And taste? "The chromatic play, the way the details are bound together, the nature of the fabrics all make the dressed body into a sort of 'table' laden with food, a list of flavors. And at times, when you observe photographs of the details of items of clothing by Versace, separated from the overall reference points of the body and the model, they really do look like 'dishes' of nouvelle cuisine," writes Calabrese.

Giusy Ferré, reporting in *L'Europeo*, took the opportunity to ask Calabrese a question no one else had dared to pose. Are Versace's clothes vulgar, she wondered? The semiotician replied: "I'd say yes, so long as it's understood that by that term I don't mean common. Rather, he's being provocative. First of all, he forces us to accept the idea that the designer's role is to show and to show off, whatever ideas we may have about the artist's presumed discretion. And then, he gets involved without any of that fear that all those good souls have of getting their hands dirty. After all, Caravaggio also went looking for his models among the crowds in the markets."

On June 13 Versace opened his most magnificent boutique yet, at number 62 Faubourg Saint-Honoré, not far from the Elysée Palace in Paris. Near the Parisian temples of fashion belonging to Saint Laurent, Lacroix, Lagerfeld and Hermès, Versace had bought and rehabbed 1,200 square meters on three floors of an elegant 1932 building, spending $9 million. Architects Rocco Magnoli and Lorenzo Carmellini were in charge of restoring the building. Versace himself supervised the interior decor—"Visconti-esque" according to *Le Figaro*—with mosaics, neoclassical murals, trompe-l'oeil caryatids and draperies of steel and crystal. The sheer ambition seemed astonishing to many, especially as the moment wasn't very favorable for international fashion, with profits declining, advertising investments down and the cost of labor high. Despite all this, the Versace group continued to grow. As Santo Versace told Enrico Arosio in *L'Espresso*, their sales would exceed 700 billion lire in 1991. They could count 120 boutiques and mono-label sales points around the world, and 320 total sales points. In Japan alone, Versace had 60 billion lire worth of sales. "We will continue to produce in Italy," Santo stressed, "just as Mercedes does in Germany. Our bank debt is less than 3 percent of our direct and indirect sales, and we expect to bring that down to zero by January 1992."

If sales were so strong, why change anything? And in fact, Gianni Versace did not change anything. Instead, he once again cranked his neo-Baroque style up a notch. His show in June presenting his menswear collection for summer 1992 was a hit. The forty models who followed each other down the runway wore shirts in loud-colored fantasy prints, tight jeans in black-and-white diamond patterns or drawings of grotesques—even rhinestone spangles—and they sported zipped-up black leather jackets and Texan boots with silver toe caps. Over the top? Maybe, but the public was enthusiastic about this super-sexy, cocky designer, so much so that they gave him a standing ovation. Amy Spindler, writing in the *Daily News Record*, devoted to menswear, dedicated a long article to Versace under the headline "Good-time Gianni." In it, she quoted Paul Beck on the economic prospects for men's clothing; he told her that the sales of Versace menswear had grown 30 percent the previous season, when they had opened their doors to the buyers just two days after the first Gulf War began. She asked Versace if the establishment continued to bore him as much as it always had. He replied: "Yes, I'm deeply bored by that terribly old-fashioned Wall Street executive look. I want to see a man who puts imagination and creativity into the way he *dresses*, just to please himself." Spindler observed that Versace's philosophy could be the title of a pop song by one of the rock stars who wore his clothes. Versace said: "Why put a gray jacket on when your ego is already gray? Why not shine? Who needs another beige suit in this moment?" And in that moment, when Milan looked particularly gray to the reporter from the *Daily News Record*, men decked out with Versace's trimmings seemed definitely newsworthy.

But his Atelier collection show in Paris on July 20 was, well, over the top. This time as never before Versace saw his clothes attacked. The *International Herald Tribune* defined his look as "sexpot" and reported a comment from a U.S. buyer: "It's *hot* couture but it's sure not haute couture." "Versace Provides the Razzle and Lacroix the Dazzle in Paris" headlined *The New York Times*, while *Women's Wear Daily*, somewhat more indulgent, conceded that certain of his baby-doll dresses might signal a new vein of less aggressive seduction for Versace. *Carnet parisien* went so far as to write about luxury call girls. Versace brought out eleven of the hottest and most beautiful models of the moment—Christy Turlington, Claudia Schiffer, Carla Bruni—who stunned the audience with hyper-sexy body stockings, their long legs folded into tall black boots à la *Pretty Woman*.

Gianni Versace was not a man to take criticism lightly. He fought back. "The most recent offensive against me came at the Paris haute couture shows, when some of the press called the clothes made in my atelier vulgar," he told Maria Vittoria Carloni in *Panorama*. "And meanwhile in my Faubourg Saint-Honoré shop there was a mob of women trying on dresses and the orders and reservations for clothes and accessories were pouring in. By now it should be obvious to all that a runway show is a provocation; it means taking certain ideas to extremes— in other words, it's a performance, a *show*. Something like a game, that unfortunately can very quickly turn ugly." When the journalist asked him how he reconciled the need to wow people with the stability of the brand and the salability of the clothes, he replied: "There are designers who work primarily under license, lending their name and their work to others. And then there are those who put on wild runway shows that everyone talks about but then go out and produce clothes that are very different, produce what are called the classics. And so in the stores you find boring, well-made clothes that share no more than the label with the designer's brand. To my mind, the classics are something else."

What the classics are Versace would demonstrate on October 6, when the Milan prêt-à-porter shows opened at his Via Gesù headquarters. Dispensing altogether with the runway and using just five models, he brought out his Signature collection, the first chapter in a catalogue of Versace classics whose irresistible popularity would continue to grow for the next thirteen years. "I didn't just wake up one morning with the crazy idea that I would add another extravagant collection to my work, which I think is already pretty extravagant," he said. "The idea derives from the fact that people come into one of my stores— and by now there are thirty-five of them under our management around the world—and for example, they ask for a sweater in silk and cashmere, maybe a model from last year or two years ago. Or perhaps a blazer or a shirt that's no longer on sale." Signature would be the collection of his best-selling items. The first, for spring-summer 1992, was made up of some thirty printed silk shirts to pair with raincoat jackets in pastel colors, shorts and golden-tinted bloused dresses. There were many styles of foulard, one dedicated to Elton John. The prints were those on his best-selling clothes, but in fresh colors of white, sky blue and rose. They were the same colors he would show in his ready-to-wear collection four days later, worn, as always, by his beloved supermodels.

His watchword was still the neo-Baroque. But this time Versace's renowned prints were married to a different color palette. "I've added something new," he told Maria Vittoria Carloni in *Panorama*. "I've used a lot of white, sky blue and rose, the colors of a Lolita of the 19th century," he said. The formula: long skirts, miniskirts and very short dresses from under which peek malicious hems and underskirts of tulle and lace. All were worn with masculine-cut jean shirts, leather belts with buckles that emphasized the waist, and richly decorated shoes and jewelry. Versace also presented a new print pattern based on marine motifs—corals, shells and starfish—that were stamped onto long, clingy dresses and skin-tight jumpsuits to give them color and pizzazz. The show was the triumph that Versace had more or less come to expect and earned him attention well beyond the fashion world. The prominent advertising executive Emanuele Pirella, for example, declared that "we must all be grateful to these designers who, even as literature and the visual arts decline, are keeping style alive. Carlo Emilio Gadda[1] is dead; art is dead. But the Baroque lives on in Versace's shows."

When the fashion shows were over, Versace flew around the globe to Japan, taking his whole family with him, to launch his *Fashion for Thought* exhibit, which had been so influential two years earlier in Italy. On display at the Kobe art museum looking out onto the bay were dozens of items of clothing, accessories, couture pieces,

---

1. Gadda was a Milanese-born 20th-century writer celebrated for his baroque style.

jewelry and drawings, along with, obviously, Versace's costumes designed for the theater. The exhibit was popular in Japan not only with fashionistas, but also with the general public, who flocked to see it. His stay in Japan allowed Versace to consolidate his market share in that Far Eastern country, which then represented 16 percent of the brand's sales. "Japan is a fairly mature market for us," Santo told the press in those days. "Meanwhile we expect to double our earnings in the rest of the Far East in the next three years."

And that wasn't all. When Santo and Gianni returned from their Japanese trip, the sales rankings for the sector spoke loud and clear: Gianni Versace was at the top of the list in sales among the designers and stood twentieth in the ranking of Italian clothing and textile companies. "With this rate of growth, we could be in the top ten in a couple of years," Santo told *L'Espresso*. "Despite the scarce competitiveness of Italian industry, Versace is a company run with courage. And then, between 1988 and 1991, we've invested more than 160 billion lire in the commercial network and the industrial sector."

Versace ended the year with four aces, earning his fourth Occhio d'Oro prize, having won the award for best Italian designer in 1982, 1985 and 1990. A jury of international experts handed him the prize in December. The press on both sides of the Atlantic chimed in with headlines like "Versace's Still the Best." Prize statue in hand, Gianni could not resist a small barb in the direction of his critics, who more than once during the year had accused him of being vulgar.

"Vulgar? Perhaps I have simply dared. And those who dare usually obtain excellent results." The excellent results were also those of the outstanding balance sheets, which marked a year to remember: direct and indirect sales reached 700 billion lire. Gianni and Santo's sly year-end comment: "Up until now we've just been having fun. But in the future we intend to have even more fun."

CHAPTER 14
Bondage Girls

January 1992. Worry pervaded the men's fashion shows in Milan, showing ready-to-wear for winter 1992–1993. The word "slump," up until now an utter taboo, had begun to circulate insistently within the fashion industry. In *l'Unità*, Gianluca Lo Vetro commented on the economic picture: "The clothing sector registered a sharp upswing in imports of some 44 percent (for a total of 1,920 billion lire) against an extremely modest rise in exports of 5 percent (for a total of 5,866 billion lire). Certainly, the balance for the sector continues to be positive, with total sales reaching an astronomical 16.5 trillion lire. But the golden age in which people bought a lot of, perhaps even too much, clothing appears to be over."

For just this reason, the fashion shows that season were trying for something eye-catching and unexpected— it was the easiest way to give a new shine to male fashion that had never been all that daring, despite a new trend toward informality that was seen in more than one collection. Versace did not need to do anything too spectacular, for the Versace man was already revolutionary enough. That season, Versace offered new ideas in the fabrics, one of the ways he always loved to show his creativity: vests decorated with metal chips applied with a liquid crystal technology; raised prints produced with electrostatic presses. The Versace man was wearing trousers cut like tight jeans in denim and other fabrics, and polo shirts, jean jackets and silk shirts in catchy prints. His collection seemed designed to meet the challenge the well-known sociologist Giuseppe De Rita had tossed out at a recent presentation of *Pitti Uomo*: "Be daring, so as to revive the faltering desire to be seen," (so Lucia Sollazzo in *La Stampa* summed up De Rita's remarks). Versace also had a guest of honor at his show: his friend Elton John, who that May would go on a world tour for which Gianni would design not only the costumes but the sets and the lights.

At the end of January, the great corruption scandals known as Tangentopoli ("Bribesville") that would rock Italy's business and political worlds, began to break. The "Clean Hands" judicial investigation opened its books, and the designers, all of them, were drawn into the vortex of inspections and controls. In Versace's headquarters and home on Via Gesù in Milan, the tax and customs police confiscated 170 antiquities from the designer's collection. Versace, in Miami to supervise an advertising campaign, remained unruffled. "I can only thank the archaeological superintendence. This way I'll have a perfect catalogue of my collection done up by them." Santo, back in Milan, also sounded unworried: "We have nothing to hide. We're used to having the tax police come around. They come every January to inspect our books. Now they'll be able to work at their leisure on all the pieces of marble that my brother has bought in all these years." The pieces of marble included the columns, vases, busts and Greek and Roman statues that adorned the house on Via Gesù, most of them highlighted in the interior plan worked out by Renzo Mongiardino at Gianni's bidding. "They are all legal purchases," Santo told *Corriere della Sera*, "bought from antique dealers, most of them Italian. And Gianni's house has been photographed for various magazines. We have never tried to hide these things."

In these same days Versace's second book dedicated to the theater, *Versace Teatro: dall'Ermitage al Covent Garden*, came out in a limited edition published by Franco Maria Ricci. A collection of unpublished sketches and drawings of costumes, it testified to five years of the designer's work alongside the great masters of ballet and opera. Roy Strong, Versace's friend and long-time director of the Victoria and Albert Museum, wrote the text; Mario Pasi provided comments on each performance. In his introduction, Versace thanked Werner Bernskotter, his right-hand man for drawings, whose job it was to translate the designer's rough sketches—both the clothing designs and the theater costumes—into luxurious finished images. He also thanked Léon Bakst, the early 20th-century costumist and set designer for the Ballets Russes, with whom Versace said he felt a deep affinity. The third person he thanked was his partner Antonio, who had been working with him for some years on the theater projects and "whose presence," Versace wrote, "has been indispensable for me."

Only a few days before the March fashion shows, a dispute broke out that hit Versace hard. In an interview with Roberto Di Caro in *L'Espresso*, the designer Krizia, in life Mariuccia Mandelli, talked to the reporter about various activities to raise money for and awareness about AIDS. The immune deficiency syndrome had become the new plague of the end of the 20th century, and in Europe and America, the disease had a terrible prognosis for gays (the Hollywood movie on the subject, *Philadelphia*, would come out in 1993). Krizia told the reporter she approved of the latest controversial Benetton advertisement photographed by Oliviero Toscani, which showed the face of a young man with full-blown AIDS, close to death. She also said she approved of the discreet campaign being carried out by Valentino, while she attacked Gianni Versace and the initiative labelled Convivio—three days of fundraising for the Italian Association for the Battle Against AIDS scheduled to take place in June. Krizia, who had read headlines in the newspapers like "Versace Calls Celebrities to Action Against AIDS," wasn't enthusiastic about Versace's project.

"I think it's crazy to spend a lot of money to stage a celebrity event that's in bad taste and for which 80 percent of the proceeds will be spent on stands, public relations and princely dinners. It would be a lot simpler to decide that all of us in the fashion business will give a certain sum—maybe a large sum—for the fight against AIDS, without asking any ambiguous returns in terms of image."

The idea had come to Versace walking down the streets of New York, when he visited Seventh On Sale, a market with proceeds to go to charity sponsored by *Vogue* America. Struck by the event, he decided he wanted to bring its spirit and organization to Italy. So on his return to Italy he called Franca Sozzani, his friend and editor in chief of *Vogue Italia*, who managed to get most of the Italian and international designers to donate some nice items from their collections to put on sale at half price for the charity event.

Just as the disagreement between the two designers seemed about to turn nasty, Santo Versace stepped in to calm the waters with a diplomatic reply to Krizia: "The participation in our initiative is practically universal, beginning with Giorgio Armani, Valentino Garavani and Gianfranco Ferré. The idea was Gianni's, yes, but no more than the idea because he himself and we as a company immediately took a step back and it is the Italian Association for the Battle Against AIDS who are the sponsors of Convivio. They supply the organization; they supply the people who are managing the project. Versace is one among many here, none of us is running the show. We're all working together and it's the first time we have seen this happen in the fashion world. Working to provide three days of music, fashion and performance, in which anyone can participate, no matter how much they earn, from those who pay a million lire a head for the dinner, to those who spend 5,000 lire for a ticket to enter the market."

Convivio indeed took place, as Gianni had so intensely wished. "Gianni was a machine, a volcano in eruption," recalls Dr. Mauro Moroni, an infectious disease specialist and chairman of the Lombardy branch of the Italian Association for the Battle Against AIDS. "In the briefest possible period of time he convinced all the Italian and international designers to donate items from their collections for the event. And that's not all. Gianni would sit and listen to us for hours as we discussed the medical and public health aspects of the problem; he always wanted to be informed. And when someone asked him why he had started up Convivio, he would say that it was only in this way that his name and his fame meant anything. I remember the gala supper the first time it was held, at Castello Sforzesco, when we had a thousand VIP guests. Well, there was a lot of rivalry in that crowd, and disagreement, and Gianni was sitting with Armani, Valentino and Ferré. With a smile on his face I'll never forget. But do you know when he smiled the most? When we told him how much money we had collected." The first Convivio earned the very respectable sum of 1.6 billion lire, and the amount nearly doubled in 1994—and rose to 2.7 million euros at the 2006 event.

In March, the fall-winter 1992–1993 ready-to-wear shows mostly offered a "sensible" look, with miniskirts momentarily absent in favor of pants, calf-lengths, bloused tops of finely constructed leather, big skirts in leopard spots and embroidered evening wear. There was nothing outrageous, but precisely because it was a difficult moment, Italian designers pulled out all the creative talent and high craftsmanship they are capable of. Versace, however, wasn't playing the game. This time he sent out a collection that would be considered his most scandalous, inspired by the British artist Allen Jones and his sculptures of S&M girls. Versace's clothes would earn the term "bondage fashion," because the gorgeous models sheathed in long black dresses cinched with silk or leather belts dressed up with golden buckles, or pressed into tiny bodices latched with diamond clasps and wearing black chokers and high black leather boots with stiletto heels, inevitably evoked sadomasochistic sex games. Natalia Aspesi, in *la Repubblica*, wrote: "Closer to Almudena Grandes' Lulù than the Marquis de Sade's Justine, Versace's marvelous, dangerous porno-girl closed this year's high fashion fashion week on Wednesday night, leaving us ready for a winter that, after his show, looks far less sensible, far less thoughtful and far more menacing. His runway was invaded by women much too beautiful and ever so shameless, insolent motorcyclists, girl rodeo riders whose prey is men, wielders of the whip practiced in ruthlessness, incarnations of every dark fantasy...."

Michele Giglio, the owner of one of Italy's prime designer boutiques in Palermo, recalls Versace's "extreme" show that year: "It was as though you had been punched in the solar plexus, even stronger than the usual shock you felt after a show by Gianni. You always needed a few minutes to recover, and then you would feel convinced, once again, that he was the only real creative force in the business. The themes of his sado-maso collection were later taken up by everybody, from Gaultier to Galliano. Certainly, it wasn't an easy collection. But when we put those clothes from the runway in our shop window, the cars on the street outside would screech to a halt and curious women would come in. And then, Versace's bravura lay in the way he could take that striking item and dilute it, dissolve it into ten other versions that would sell like crazy because they had his fashion edge but not the extremism shown on the runway."

In any case, the collection was an extraordinary success, completely overturning the premise on which Italy's clothing industry was based—that the woman of today was a nice, attractive, well-turned-out lady, careful about prices and good quality, inclined to purchase clothes for the long run, and therefore nothing extravagant, in search of sobriety and an image that would reinforce her own self-respect and that of men. Versace was the first to understand what sociologist Francesco Morace argued, that "in this phase, a garment cannot be merely timely, new; it must offer cultural and emotional depth and points of reference." Perhaps that's why there were a lot of parties in the discotheques after fashion week, to counterbalance an overall look that was less than effervescent that year, to counter the rebound of Paris, where the Minister of Culture Jack Lang had helped the designers work together to offer journalists and buyers that atmosphere of glamour that fashion cannot do without.

Gianni Versace had always known this. He was the first to do fashion shows and parties with a pop-rock soundtrack. After his scandalous collection he and Donatella and Santo invited 2,000 people to party at City Square, a New York–style club where they danced to the rap beat of Black Machine. Bankers, soccer players, the Milan in-crowd, friends like Ornella Vanoni and rock stars like David Byrne stayed up all night, and even heard Naomi Campbell come to the microphone to sing.

Puritan America, however, was not so happy about the bondage girls. In November, while Gianni was in New York to open the show "Gianni Versace Signature" (a U.S. version of the exhibit *L'abito per pensare*) at the Fashion Institute of Technology, the press asked him about his most recent collection. The Style section of *The New York Times* led off with a long article about the Versace "bondage collection" under the headline "Chic or Cruel?" The article highlighted the opinions of Holly Brubach, the fashion critic at *The New Yorker*, who said, "There were people who loved it, who thought it was brilliant, the greatest thing he had ever done. And others of us, mostly women, could barely evaluate the design aspect of it because we were so offended. I have to say that I hated it…. Versace's designs, more than anyone else's, suggest specific sexual practices. They strike me as needing equipment.

"Versace riles women who think this is exploitative and appeals to women who think of his dominatrix look as a great Amazonian statement. It could go either way. Either the Versace woman is wielding the whip, or she's the one who's harnessed and being ridden around the room wearing a collar and a leash."

But Versace, according to Maria Giulia Minetti in *Epoca*, only smiled at such criticisms. In any case, feminist author Naomi Wolf, quoted in the same article in the *Times*, said, "I don't feel necessarily that S&M metaphors in fashion are innately degrading. It depends on the context, on who's wearing it, what it's saying."

And above all, the two pages of polemics in *The New York Times* only underlined Versace's undisputed success. And what about all the socialites wearing bondage fashion at the mid-September Rock 'n' Rule charity ball at the Park Avenue Armory, with which Gianni opened Piazza Italia? This fashion and culture extravaganza under the wing of the Italian Foreign Trade Bureau was dedicated to the 500th anniversary of Columbus's visit to America. Their fashion choices certainly gave Gianni a boost.

That evening, at the party for the Gianni Versace Signature exhibition opening, Gianni stood in front of the restaurant Le Madri, where Anna Wintour of *Vogue* had invited a hundred friends in his honor. He was smiling and relaxed. According to Minetti, "Holly Brubach has written him a letter of a page and a half that begins like this: 'Dear Gianni, I'm absolutely mortified about the article in the *Times*. My views were brutally altered, and in some cases, completely invented.'…"

Meanwhile, the Versace brand continued to prosper. "Intelligent marketing operations have highlighted and put order in the exuberant talent of Gianni Versace," wrote Giusy Ferré in *L'Europeo*. "It begins with haute couture, Atelier, and runs down the line to Signature, launched last season for classics; Couture, for prêt-à-porter that is partly finished by hand, then Versus, Jeans, Jeans Couture…."

"They offer various degrees of finishing," said Santo Versace, "and are priced accordingly. But there's an underlying design hand, that of my brother and sister Gianni and Donatella, who are responsible for an immense amount of work. Is there an economic downturn? Between hard work and new ideas, we don't feel it at the moment. We were at 620 billion lire in indirect sales in 1990, and we expect to touch 910 billion this year."

In those years—amid the evanescent disputes about his style and a turnover that couldn't have been more solid—Gianni first fell in love with Miami: the south Florida city, but more precisely the spit of land across the causeway with its beaches of fine white sand that run up the coast for more than five miles, with the world's most amazing collection of Art Deco buildings, decked with palms, hibiscus and bougainvillea. Miami Beach: a tropical paradise. The first to go there in the 1980s "were New York yuppies, beginning around 1986, eager to cop a tan and wanting some downtime to cope with the stress of Manhattan," Pino Buongiorno described the trend in *Panorama*. "Rather than launch themselves into the traffic for two hours on Friday night to reach the Hamptons or Connecticut, they would take a flight at about six p.m., landing about two and a half hours later in time for dinner at Polly Magoo, owned by two Genoese restaurateurs, Paolo Secondo and Pietro Pagano, who had started up the famous Tre Merli in Manhattan. They could then spend the rest of the evening at the Loft or Warsaw, two hip discotheques, or have a last beer in one of the many bars along the beach where they play live jazz and reggae."

Gianni went to Miami with Antonio D'Amico so they could meet Melissa De Sardinia, owner of the Versace shop at Bal Harbour, the shopping district ten minutes north of Miami Beach. "We had planned on going on to Cuba," D'Amico recalls, "but Gianni wanted to stay in Miami. He was mesmerized by Ocean Drive, the street with the clubs that runs along the beach, by the houses painted in pastel colors, and above all, by the people: sixty-year-olds sporting rollerblades, black ladies with umbrellas under the sun on the lawn in front of the sea, fathers with their children, muscular young male models. It was an incredible mix of people in a chaotic world. We stayed there in a little hotel, the Flamingo, and there was a pink Cadillac from the fifties parked out front. Right away Gianni wanted to see the houses for sale in South Beach. And he fell in love with a building that was just two streets behind the hotel—a three-story house that was called Amsterdam Palace or Casa Casuarina, after a type of maritime pine, and built in sandstone on the model of the Alcazar de Colòn, Christopher Columbus's family house in Santo Domingo. Gianni said, 'If I'm going to buy a house here, it's going to be this one.' And that's just what happened. Less than a month later, Gianni had sent Giovanni Travia, who looked after our business affairs under Santo, to buy it. Then Gianni bought a falling-down old hotel painted gray next door, earning us the protests of the local citizenry who wanted to preserve it as it was, given that the whole neighborhood was under historic preservation to protect the thirties buildings in the Deco District. And he made an annex out of it."

The American press calculated that Gianni paid less than $3 million for Casa Casuarina—1,240 square meters over its three floors—when he bought it from its

American owner, Gerry Sanchez. Here in Miami the idea of his new collection, the Home Collection, first came to the designer. "Versace had begun to think about decorating his house in Miami even before he rehabbed it," says Patrizia Cucco. "Down there under the tropical sun, he would need strong designs and violent colors. Exactly the ones that he used in his prints, which were a great success. That's how Versace's Home Collection came to be: out of his search for something new, different from the usual prints for home decorating. Cushions—we sold millions of those and they became cult objects. And then there were the first services in porcelain; in fact it was Rosenthal's artistic director himself who came to Gianni and asked him to work with them. Gianni was delighted. And he designed four different patterns in a single season, violating every marketing rule—Medusa, Marco Polo, Re Sole and Barocco. Four patterns that could be mixed up. So that you could set the table with four different patterns at each place setting—an idea that soon became a trend."

From Miami to London. There, in the heart of one of the world's great shopping districts, at 34 Old Bond Street, Versace opened an elegant new shop on May 30. The word "shop" was by now inadequate to describe these new emporiums, which under the Versace insignia were more rightly termed palaces. The London location was a stately four stories, 700 square meters of marble in ten different colors, plaster cornices, gilt, silver, mirrors and lighting effects worthy of the stage. Versace spent $10 million to decorate it. According to Paolo Filo della Torre, writing in *la Repubblica*, "Austere Old Bond Street has been transformed into a sort of Via Veneto, where celebrities, socialites, soubrettes and playboys, famous actors, big-name singers, half-naked models and hip aristocrats walk like peacocks down the street to the joy of the throngs of paparazzi who have staked out every corner." Inside, the glossy guests included Ivana Trump, Elton John, Kylie Minogue, Britt Ekland and Joan Collins and also such designers as Vivienne Westwood and Bruce Oldfield, who provided Princess Diana's clothes.

"The pleasurable surprise at this party," Filo della Torre went on, "is the strange mix of guests. Among the big names here is the editor in chief of *The Independent*, Andreas Whittam Smith. The kind of man who in the past would have been considered too serious, too sober for such an event. But obviously the fantastic luxury that Versace has brought to Bond Street exerts its fascination on him, too."

It was true, Versace was at the height of his fascination; his clothes and accessories, at the leading edge of fashion, were being copied everywhere. "There's no secret to our success," said Santo Versace about Gianni Versace S.p.A., the holding company of what had become a huge family group, in an interview with Daniela Giancristofaro in *Uomini e business*. "The only 'secret' we have is our courage, and then work, work, work. We're not people who panic when there's a slump in the fashion business. We've simply continued to follow what was always our number one rule: to produce collections in which Gianni's creative genius, the price of the products and the service to clients are three carefully balanced elements. If we add to that the fact that in recent seasons Gianni has matured in an extraordinary way because the company has allowed him to give free rein to his 'creative madness,' and the fact that our company is by now a genuine industrial group that can take risks because we have a solid organization at our backs, well, I suppose I've revealed to you the secret of our success."

So it was another good year. But with a litigious interval. The two princes of the fashion shows, Giorgio Armani and Gianni Versace, had scheduled their presentations at Milano Collezioni on the same day at the same time, seven-thirty p.m. on October 8. Both of them wanted to celebrate the grande finale of fashion week. The dispute went on for days and neither wanted to yield. Finally Rosanna Armani, Giorgio's sister, and Santo Versace met with Beppe Modenese and came up with a solution. The label with the Medusa logo would show at six-thirty p.m., while Armani's collection would go out at nine p.m. The quarrel was the subject of days of reporting in the papers, ending with the classic declarations of harmony from the two contenders, who denied there was ever any disagreement in the first place. Finally, October arrived and the lights shone on the runways. To counter the economic downturn, designers had promised to bring out clothes that would amaze and astonish buyers and fashionistas. Versace succeeded fully at this and his collection was called 'revolutionary.' "These are years of change," Gianni told the journalists. "There's a lot of energy and a lot of fun in this collection."

In the end, the clothes told the story. They were "country" style, distinctly hippie and redolent of the open air, colors and freedom—Provençal prints and bell-bottomed pants. But Versace's version of hippie was "a whimsical neo-hippie deluxe" that included his celebrated prints to spruce up folk-style dresses, skirts and pants, with plenty of accessories. On the runway, Naomi, Linda and Marpessa sported generous décolletés à la Sophia Loren, and seventies-style shirts tied under the bosom. There was never anything nostalgic about Versace's clothes; his neo-hippies were strong and sensual, they were "commanding women." And then there were the items inspired by Miami, underwear styles, tight as a second skin and showing nipple, as well as unusual vests like tailcoats. The music that provided the background to the collection was all about mixing genres: the resounding "Panis Angelicus" sung by Sting and Luciano Pavarotti, matched with tapes by Lenny Kravitz, Nirvana and Guns N' Roses.

The year 1992 closed in high gear. Versace learned he would be awarded the CDFA Prize of the Council of Fashion Designers of America, the *de facto* Oscar of fashion, in New York. It was the award's first presentation, and it went unanimously to Versace. Afterwards, Giorgio Armani would also get the prize. The story of the long-running rivalry between the two burst out in the press once again. In December, *Time* dedicated two profiles to the two designers, under the headlines, "Hot Gianni" and "Cool Giorgio." Writing about Versace, *Time* celebrated his show at the Fashion Institute of Technology and spoke of "the talent and creativity of the god of Italian fashion." About Armani, the news magazine wrote of his "innate elegance, the sumptuous but sober style of his evening clothes in his recent collections and the entrepreneurial skills of Italian fashion."

Although he was pleased about the recognition he had received, Versace ended the year on a note of unease. He confided to Renzo Magosso in *Gente*, "It's a moment of crisis for me. Not that crisis is negative, for it brings with it change and novelty. In the end, I don't think it's right to close yourself up in an ivory tower, even though it means you are safe and protected. To create is also to risk. If I had never taken a chance, I would never have shown the clothes that everyone loves today. Believe me: to avoid risk is also to die a little. And I love life very much."

CHAPTER 15
Miami

Something was changing. In Milan's little shopping quadrilateral where the best clothing stores are located, the January 1993 sales, which had already begun before Christmas, were offering discounts up to 80 percent. A few months previously, Italy had reluctantly devalued the lira and taken it out of the European Monetary System. This gave the Italian economy and especially the textiles and clothing sector a welcome breath of oxygen in terms of increased exports. But while the balance of trade was positive for Italy, employment rates were plunging. Big companies surrendered to bank management; small and medium ones were failing, and quite a few had to lay off workers. Many producers in the clothing business began to delocalize, moving part of their production to countries with lower wages. In France the economic crisis in the luxury sector was even worse than in Italy. Grunge—the dress style favored by Seattle youth—was beginning to arrive from the U.S. Flannel shirts, shapeless sweaters, used Levi's, well-worn sweatshirts and T-shirts had shown up in New Yorker Perry Ellis's collections and quickly become a style. It was a signal that fashion had turned once again to the street for inspiration—to people and what was happening in the world.

Versace called Avedon. Following their years of artistic cooperation that had given Versace's clothes their edge and image, their paths had parted. Avedon was ever more caught up with his exhibits and his books, Versace ever more intent on pumping up female seductiveness and aggressiveness. "By now women have accomplished what they want," he told Maria Vittoria Carloni in *Panorama*. "They're strong, they don't need to dress like men. They've won, and therefore they can go back to being simple. And the new simplicity in fashion goes along with a classic image, like Avedon's." Avedon, in turn, said, "I'm a slave of quality, an addict of perfection. I can only work with people of superior quality. In advertising, Versace. In the media world, *The New Yorker*. And in fact the magazine's new editor in chief Tina Brown had just nominated Avedon official photographer for the sophisticated weekly. In early February, the magazine ran an advertising special with Avedon's photos for Versace. They shot the campaign in Manhattan in a former candy factory on the Hudson that had been transformed into a photographer's studio. White sand and a huge piece of driftwood were trucked in from Montauk Bay. The spirit of the campaign revolved around the regeneration of female beauty, interpreted by Naomi Campbell, Stephanie Seymour, Christy Turlington, Kristen McMenamy and an as-yet unripe 17-year-old, Kate Moss.

A month later Versace was back in New York to receive his statuette for international designer of the year from the Council of Fashion Designers of America. *Le tout* New York—fashion, the media, the film world—descended on Lincoln Center for the awards ceremony. Elton John handed the prize to Versace, "a friend," he says, "whose creativity I appreciate," while Karl Lagerfeld heralded Steven Meisel, the photographer for Madonna's book *Sex* and the pygmalion of all the latest glossy beauties. Awards also went to Marc Jacobs, designer at Perry Ellis and the guru of grunge, and Donna Karan, who received the award for menswear from Giorgio Armani.

When the fashion shows rolled around in March, the designers didn't seem all that worried about economic downturn. "Italian fashion," said Armani, "when you look beyond the current situation, is both solid and secure. We are the only ones in the world who know how to produce quality ideas and clothing." Versace, too, was serene and unruffled by the economic circumstances, declaring his pre-collection sales were up 20 percent for fall-winter 1993. His show, "dedicated to women who work," included a lot of knits (the new best sellers that season, following the grunge trend) and a new style of sheath that fell to the ground, but in stretch fabric, to pair with everything—jackets, overcoats. These were down-to-earth clothes, worn for the first time by very young models, adolescents. There was, however, some nervousness about the economy even among the designers, who, when challenged, closed ranks in defense of each other.

Inside the fashion world the buzz that year was about the fact that Suzy Menkes—the influential fashion editor of the *International Herald Tribune* who lived in Paris and was partial to French fashion—had been excluded from the Versace show because she had criticized his Atelier collection when it came out in the French capital. Santo Versace, talking about that review, said, "We accept criticism, we live in a democracy, but we also insist on respect for our work, which can't be attacked in a biased way." Ferré barred Menkes from his show for the same reason, because she had practically ignored the Dior collection that he designed. Perhaps to back her up, the British paper *The Guardian* went after Versace for his use of supermodels in his shows. It was all exhibitionism and spectacle, the paper wrote. Furthermore, when their correspondent in Milan sent Versace a written question, he had replied, "Recession is for fools, not for people who work." *The Guardian* read that high-handed quip as the response of a Renaissance prince and compared him to a Borgia, no less. Versace, in reply, said the journalist had just made the whole thing up. And he added, perhaps a bit ingenuously, "In London, as in Paris and many other cities, when I opened my boutique, it was a great success. If others fail, it certainly isn't my fault."

The English might be caustic, but the Americans continued to love Italian style. At the Oscar ceremony in Los Angeles, most of the stars were dressed by Italian designers, whom the newspapers have dubbed the "cappuccino boys." Whatever. Although Armani won the Oscar night contest, followed by Valentino, Versace made a good showing; Cindy Crawford wore one of his dresses (on the arm of Richard Gere, wearing Armani), and

Sylvester Stallone, Jane Fonda and Jeff Bridges also sported Versace.

Versace's love affair with America was going strong, strong, strong. Even before he finished the rehab of Casa Casuarina in Miami (directed by architect Thierry Moore and builder Wallace Tutt) Versace and Donatella joined forces to produce a book about the city, *South Beach Stories*, with Leonardo Arte. It became a cult book. A stunning production in best Versace style, the book summed up the spirit of this San Tropez of the year 2000 in a wildly eclectic mix of images—groups of models in loud printed shirts, outfits of black leather covered with studs, bathing suits with a greca motif, vacationers among the palms who smile happily in front of the camera. It showed Christy Turlington and Kate Moss on the beach or at the café wearing Versace jumpsuits and bathing suits, right next to lots of black-and-white photos of Donatella with Paul Beck and their children Allegra and Daniel— happy moments in a family photo album. There were shots of the beach, the Cadillacs, the pool, the ocean. Doug Ordway, a rising young photographer who was also crazy about Miami, spent two months putting together this reportage. The book was sprinkled with sketches by Manuela Brambatti, Gianni's colleague from 1981 who made up the drawings of his clothes in strong lines and bright colors, and with the spirited drawings of Alighiero Boetti and Thierry Perez. The text consisted of ten tales by Marco Parma (in real life Paolo Petroni, fashion magazine editor and author of the book *Sotto il veste niente*) peopled by extreme characters—the ex-prize fighter, the Native American dancer—who have found their lost identity in Miami.

When Versace presented his book at Bloomingdale's in New York, the 600 copies he brought with him sold in a flash, the proceeds devolving to the Italian Association for the Battle Against AIDS. The super-athletic, hyper-vitaminized models of *South Beach Stories*, however, would already have vanished just a few months later when Versace showed off his menswear collections for summer 1994. The designer announced he wanted a new direction—and a new direction it was. The runway disappeared and the male models were arranged in tableaux vivants in the garden of the Via Gesù headquarters, transformed for the occasion into a sort of tropical paradise. They were wearing shirts of pink or lace, pullovers of punched leather, sweaters as wide open as fishnets, fabrics that were stressed and slashed. The men were less macho and more adolescent now, following the new ad campaign photographed by Bruce Weber whose models were young college kids, or guys like the 22-year-old champion California swimmer who posed as an archer on a horse in a famous photo.

At Gianni Versace, the word was a "neo-romantic" look, inspired, perhaps, by a new brand of pacifism in society. But this time, Donatella was most invested in this definition; she had become ever more involved in connecting the clothes with the Versace image. Gianni was by now already absorbed in a project that Mario Mafucci, an executive at RAI-TV channel one, had proposed to him, a sort of reportage-happening during fashion week in Paris. It would cover Versace's Atelier show and Karl Lagerfeld's show for Chanel, starring supermodels like Naomi Campbell, Carla Bruni and Claudia Schiffer as well as Versace's friends attending the shows (Sting, Elton John, Adam Clayton of U2, Anna Oxa) and the glamorous crowd assembled for Chanel, all to be shown in prime time on July 27. The idea for this special came from Gianni, who asked that Karl Lagerfeld be a participant. "I didn't want to have to be the only one holding up a program of an hour and a half. Karl is a friend. And I also asked that Christian Lacroix be included." The two designers commented on each others' shows, and Versace took part in the complex editing phase of the program, to make sure all went well.

This time Atelier really won Paris over. Once again Versace sent his supermodels out on the runway—among them the Czech model Eva Herzigova—wearing jackets in stressed fabrics, suits made of slashed tweed covered by spiderwebs of lace, gorgeously finished slips and camisoles, minidresses with side slits, and stretch satin velvet stockings with inserts of lace and embroidery, "because women," Versace would say, "haven't accepted long skirts and don't want to cover themselves up in men's dressing gowns." In his audience were Elton John, Pedro Almodóvar, the transsexual Bibi Andersen, Vincent Perez, Roman Polanski and Emmanuelle Seigner, who applauded vigorously every time an item came out and convinced Janie Samet of *Le Figaro* that "the prescription that Dr. Versace has written to cure our lack of appetite for fashion and all the rest was great fun." Versace's show at the Ritz had by now become a genuine happening, followed by little clouds of photographers and TV cameramen from around the world. To any who argued that Versace had made fashion into too much of a spectacle, he replied that since he began showing in Paris he had multiplied his production five times and was besieged with requests for cinema and theater costumes.

Meanwhile across the ocean in Miami, environmental activists were stirring up a campaign against Versace, a campaign that made the national press. They opposed his plans to tear down the Revere Hotel, the ugly fifties building that Gianni had bought along with Casa Casuarina in order to install his offices and guest house. Although the restored sites promised to be glamorous in true Versace style and thus would enhance the appeal of the Miami's Deco District, and despite the glitzy homage paid to the place by Gianni in his *South Beach Stories*, the hardliners for the preservation of the status quo managed to block the project. But then the dispute died down, because it turned out that Versace had the right to tear down the hotel since the city ordinance only protected buildings put up through the year 1949. The mayor of Miami took Versace's side, and in the end, the Miami Design Preservation League went so far as to ask him to join their committee.

On the business front, even Versace now had to keep an eye on his finances. The problem of the moment was Japanese demand, for although the Japanese had filled up their wardrobes with Italian fashion in past years, now, with their economy in recession, they were holding onto their yen. As chairman of Gianni Versace S.p.A., Santo Versace had been working out a plan of action down to the tiniest details. To ward off a nasty drop in sales (which had been equivalent to about $140 million the previous year), Santo decided to cut their structural costs to the bone, folding the three companies—which in partnership with Mitsui, imported Versace lines and distributed them to the eighty-eight direct and franchise-owned sales points in Japan—into one. The overall balance sheets of Gianni Versace were, in any case, looking good. According to Daniela Giancristofaro writing in *Uomini e business*, the group's turnover in direct and indirect sales in 1992 was 910 billion lire, with net profits of 25 billion lire and a cash flow of some 44 billion. These were somewhat miraculous figures, the journalist hastened to add, taking into consideration that 1992 knocked the great majority of Italian clothing and textile producers for a loop, and that Versace's 1993 results appeared certain to repeat the group's excellent performance. Commenting on the slump in the textile sector, Santo Versace singled out tax pressure as a major cause. "In Italy," Santo told Giancristofaro, "tax pressure has now reached untenable levels. If Prime Minister Carlo Azeglio Ciampi and the Minister of Finance don't reduce it, it will be as if they were inviting us to move our activities abroad. You know, in 1992 the companies in our group reached a tax rate of nearly 53 percent? We had net profits of 25.2 billion lire and and a cash flow of 44 billion lire, but if our tax rates had been the same as in 1991, the profits and cash flow would have been 27.7 and 47 billion respectively. In one year, the state took 3 billion more in taxes. By doing that, they took away from us the means to make new investments and new hires."

Despite the country's problems, Santo Versace continued to be optimistic. "The important thing is that the state should help our companies remain competitive," he said. "Once the important markets consisted only of America, in the sense of the United States, Northern Europe and Japan. Today there's an infinite potential for the development of new markets: there's the whole Far East, there are the new Arab countries, there's Canada, China and even Mexico. The Versace group is already present in these markets. Our secret? To be good at what you do and to have a strong desire to work. But it would also be nice to have a functional Italian company at our backs."

For his October shows featuring spring-summer 1994 collections, Versace had a new surprise in store, a new trend—punk. He himself told the press: "My collection? It's going to be very punk, with a lot of black, leather and piercing, because punk is joy, it's nonconformism. It's the future, while the classic look is for hypocrites. I'd like to see everyone wearing punk. Beginning with Marella Agnelli right down to Lady Diana, whom I think would look great in a knitwear dress with holes punched in it." On October 3, when he sent his models out on the runway, the effect was shocking: black leather everything, sheaths and pullovers punched with holes, huge jeweled safety pins to rein in oversize sweaters, layers, wrinkled jackets and crazy hems. Classic items were roughed up and and tossed around to create a sort of luxury punk. Versace had once again taken that mood of laid-back-angry-young-man that you find on the streets of London and New York, and brought it into the temple of Italian fashion. Behind the clothes there was a message. This kind of laid-back punk was pacifism but without the barricades; it implied commitment and tolerance. Rips and holes were a reaction to the squalor of the political world and the whole society.

Needless to say, he also offered a huge post–fashion show party at the club Rolling Stone, with more than 2,000 invited guests, including Hollywood stars, big businessmen, supermodels, singers and intellectuals, all rigorously wearing gear with studs. The star of the evening was the American drag queen Ru Paul, a friend of Elton John. He entertained the crowd singing and doing duets, showing off, on top of his six-foot frame all wrapped in spandex, a black leather punk jacket.

The following day the press, both Italian and international (Suzy Menkes among them) applauded Versace's collection with headlines like, "Welcome Back, Punk," "Versace Likes Women Without Skirts," and "Beautiful Lolitas With Diaper Pins"—the last a reference to Naomi Campbell and Claudia Schiffer, seen in tiny minidresses from under which sprouted panties of lace and net.

But the dress that really symbolized the collection was the long, long, mermaid-look dress, open on one side and held together with enormous gilded safety pins. The black Venus Naomi Campbell wore it on the runway in an all-black version that brought down the house. The appreciation was even greater when a few months later actress Elizabeth Hurley wore the same dress for the première of *Four Weddings and a Funeral* starring her then-partner Hugh Grant. All the flash bulbs were popping for Hurley, looking so gorgeous and sexy, while the press and assembled guests all but ignored the film and the cast, so that even the sober *Financial Times*, in its account of the evening, focused on Hurley's dress, headlining its article, "The Vim and the Verve of Versace."

As November rolled around, Versace was once again deep in the show business world. This time it was film, one of his long-time passions. He designed the costumes for *Kika*, Spanish director Pedro Almodóvar's irreverent new movie, borrowing from his somewhat sixties-style spring-summer 1993 collection. The director and the designer clicked perfectly and Almodóvar's wild, sharp-edged film got a kick from the witty, over-the-top costumes Veronica Forqué wore as the sunny Kika, antagonist to Victoria Abril, dressed by Jean-Paul Gaultier.

As the year drew to a close, there was also a book: a two volume set by Versace, *Ricami e decori, decori e ricami* published by Leonardo Editore. It was something like a definitive statement of the designer's style, and rekindled the fashion world's interest in the link between Versace's creative force and the Baroque. In it, Versace's virtuoso designs mix with drawings, sketches and experiments with fabrics, with photos from his ad campaigns and paintings by Mario Schifano, Michelangelo Pistoletto and Enzo Cucchi. There's also a story by novelist and journalist Isabella Bossi Fedrigotti, who remembers Versace as a man of great curiosity. "He had asked me for a story to 'elevate' his book on embroidery. It was wonderful to talk to him because he was hungry for culture; he wanted to absorb and to learn. He was careful in choosing his words; I could feel him making an effort not to get things wrong. Interviews with designers are usually frustrating, because they answer you in clichés, they don't usually have any real interest in their interlocutor. But Versace did pay attention, he really did have that interest."

CHAPTER 16
Highs and Lows

Optimism about 1994. Gianni Versace glowed with optimism at the year-end party on December 29, 1993, that he gave in the newly splendid, just-restored Casa Casuarina to celebrate his new Miami home, the company's health and the opening of the first Versace Jeans Couture boutique. His economic prospects looked rosy: "My greatest success in recent years has been the Home Collection, which contributes 7 percent of sales," he told Maria Vittoria Carloni of *Panorama.* "In three months we've sold 10 billion lire worth of plates designed by me and produced by Rosenthal." Then he talked about his new look for the coming year, already hinted at in the Versace ad campaign by Richard Avedon. "My overall idea for 1994 is simplicity. It doesn't mean minimalism, which is so much in fashion now. I'm referring to those monk's cowls and priest's habits that deface women by trying to make them look chic when they only look miserable.... Women, fortunately, have grown mature and comfortable in their own allure. Let's leave the matter up to them. It's a sort of challenge on my part. How many women are going to rise to the challenge? Many, I hope, because it's not just a question of money. If only very few are in a position to buy couture fashion, many are in a position to recognize a style....

"And please, let's stop calling my clothes sexy. I don't repudiate anything, no, I think collections like the S&M one will continue to sell, because they represent a new direction in manners, they correspond to a time of liberation and aggressiveness for women. I don't even repudiate my decorative period—the neo-Baroque period. I've merely moved on. My book *Vanitas,* dedicated to embroidery and ornamentation marked the end of a period. But the spirit of the Baroque can still be found in my Signature collection for the home. In the end, my style has deep Italian roots linked to colors and to craftsmanship. In fashion, however, one must keep going forward, one must have the courage to do something new. I'm lucky to be able to do that with Atelier."

On January 15, Versace's Atelier collection would be shown once again at the Ritz (although Chanel had just installed a new showcase for fashion on the undergound level of the Louvre's Carrousel center). And this time Versace's look would be more pared down and essential, no doubt about it: tailored lines that looked like quotations from Balanciaga and Fortuny, a virtuoso dress as simple as a T-shirt but cut on the bias and finished with twelve different types of plissé.

And it would be a repeat performance at the fall-winter 1994 collection show in Milan. This time it was not taking place at the Milan Fair, for Versace—like Armani and Krizia—held his show at home. A ten-meter-high greenhouse with a removable roof was perched in the garden of his headquarters at Via Gesù. The steel structure had been painted a romantic garden green, like the 19th-century winter gardens at Villa Fontanelle on Lake Como, but inside the structure was equipped to provide each show with high-tech effects and lighting, to make each show as perfect as possible with supreme control of the spots. He started it with the Versus collection, and on March 1, the Gianni Versace collection. The atmosphere in the fashion world had turned euphoric again, and 1,000 journalists, 60 percent of them from abroad, along with an even larger number of buyers, jammed into Milan for the March shows.

"Downtown was an inferno of yellow taxis and black limousines, all heading for the event of the evening, the fashion show and dinner at Gianni Versace's palace," wrote Natalia Aspesi. "High-toned guests and hard-boiled journalists weak from exhaustion leapt from their cars along with buyers as magnificent as pashas, who hope rivers of gold will flow from Italian fashion. Through a tent worthy of Harun al-Rashid they entered an up-to-date version of *A Thousand and One Nights,* a crystal palace decked with satin and silk pillows in blinding colors.... After the runway show there was a sumptuous evening of dining and amnesia, as a hundred or more glitzy guests climbed up and down the Versacean palace. They went up for supper in the reception rooms, down for dessert and coffee in the designer's apartments amid archaeological remains, Empire-style furniture and paintings by artists of the Transavanguardia."

On the runway, Versace sent out his "Barbie Dolls" as Suzy Menkes dubbed the very young women who modelled alongside Linda Evangelista, Helena Christiansen, Claudia Schiffer and Nadja Auermann. They were dressed in luscious short dresses with high waists in lacquered silk or metal mesh, and tiny suits in pastel colors worn with stiletto-heeled shoes and socks pulled up over their stockings. "Versace does well to use all the top models en masse," said Giorgio Armani at the press conference before his own show. "Curves, legs and breasts on display are right for his fashion. I don't wish to castigate anyone, but I refuse to pay certain fees. It's an ethical question. There are people who live for a year on that kind of money."

But when it came to Versace's reception, everyone was there—the old rich and the new rich, the crème de la crème of international fashion journalists, actors and rock stars, among them Robert De Niro; Piersilvio Berlusconi (son of Silvio); socialite Gioia Marchi Falck; big name sociologist Francesco Alberoni; theater designer Pier Luigi Pizzi; Anna Wintour; Duran Duran; Bill Wyman of the Rolling Stones and Giulia Maria Crespi, former owner of the *Corriere della Sera*, president of the prestigious Fund for the Italian Environment, and a woman not very keen on celebrity glitz, who however once famously quipped, apropos of Milan's gloomy weather, "At least we can thank fashion!"

Business continued to be good. At the beginning of April Versace signed a new contract with Ittierre to produce and distribute the Versus and Versace Jeans

Couture lines. He also signed a new contract with them to produce part of the Signature line. The agreement, reported *Il Sole 24 ore*, would extend through the year 2000 and would cover 2 million items a year, for a total turnover of just over 1 trillion lire. Not long afterward, Gianni and Santo, Donatella and the rest of his team flew to Munich to celebrate the expansion of his store (it had opened back in 1984), redesigned so that now eleven of its fourteen shop windows faced onto the historic Odeonplatz. Two hundred guests had been invited to a reception, followed by dinner at the Trocadero with a lot of young people. The evening wound up at the P.I. disco club, where Gianni, not a great lover of late nights, left Donatella on the dance floor until the early morning. The next day he was back in Milan and for the weekend, at his beloved villa on Lake Como. On May 5 he went back up north to Berlin, where he opened a brand new store on the most elegant street in town, the Kurfürstendamm: Germany was his second most prosperous market after Italy. Rocco Magnoli and Lorenzo Carmellini, as usual, designed the huge space—600 square meters on two floors decorated with *stucco veneziano* walls, bas-relief columns, pink and blue friezes and decorations in gold leaf. There was room here for Versace's whole universe, from men's and women's prêt-à-porter to the collection for the home.

Meanwhile Santo, in Milan, was involved in negotiations with various banks. By the end of July they had to choose which international merchant bank would organize their listing on the New York Stock Exchange, planned for the following year. "We're going to offer 20 percent of the company," Santo explained, "and between now and 1997, our goal is to double our sales." They hoped the listing on Wall Street would help boost their sales in North America, then worth about 18 percent of Versace's total sales. (Europe accounted for 36 percent of sales, with Italy making up 23 percent; Japan was worth 9 percent.) The mood at Via Gesù was obviously ebullient. When Jacaranda Falck interviewed Gianni for *L'Espresso* and asked him the secret of the brand's success, he said, "It's making clothes that people want to buy. It sounds banal, but it isn't. Designers very often live in an ivory tower. I, on the other hand, like to stand on a lookout from which I can see where the world is moving. A good tailor, a good dressmaker, needs to be able to reflect the era he or she lives in. I try to get inside the mind of the modern woman. I also work, I get on and off planes all the time, I live the life of today, in short. That's why I'm able to understand the needs of my clients. I'm the only designer who doesn't just travel up and down his own runway."

A man with a huge sense of humor (and as Franca Sozzani of *Vogue Italia* once said, a man "capable also of laughing at himself"), Gianni concluded his interview with Falck with a quip. He was asked whether he agreed with Calvin Klein, who had been quoted saying that the future of fashion lay in making real clothes for real people. Versace replied: "Max Mara out of Reggio Emilia has been doing that for fifty years and he offers a product that is decidedly superior to that of Mr. Klein. If there's any sense at all left in my work, it lies in the search for the beautiful. Fashion can only survive if it continues to be a means of escapism. The dress that sells the most in my stores is the strangest one, considered unwearable by all: a slinky little punk-style sheath that's slashed and held together with safety pins. Klein? He's just an invention of the photographer Bruce Weber—a fabulous pair of underpants immortalized by a great photographer."

For his menswear collection for summer 1995, at the end of June, Versace created a performance-show, choreographed by William Forsythe of the Frankfurt Ballet, for whom Gianni had designed the costumes for the dance event *Snap Woven Effort*. He also used the occasion to tell the press about various developments in his business: that he was strengthening his control over licensing procedures, beginning with the decision to directly produce the children's wear line, previously licensed to Simint but with disappointing results; that he had purchased 75 percent of Giver Profumi and launched two new fragrances, Red Jeans for women and Blue Jeans for men. The company had also rented 3,500 square meters of space for a new showroom on Via Senato in Milan and another 700 square meters on Via Napoleone for a store selling women's lines and the home collection. Meanwhile, Gianni Versace was continuing to expand abroad, opening new shops in Los Angeles, Denver and Sydney.

When Gianni went off to Paris with the Atelier collection for the haute couture shows, the Versace circus was larger than usual. For the first time Donatella brought her two children with her: Allegra, now 8 years old, and Daniel, 3. She talked to Silvia Giacomoni of *la Repubblica* about how she thought about her role as their mother. "Allegra is like I was as a girl with my mother, who was a dressmaker and a woman of great principle. Allegra, too, has to learn that fashion is about beauty, not about frivolity. My mother taught me discipline, the difference between duty and pleasure. And I teach that to my children, too. When I'm with them, I'm one hundred percent mother." It was Donatella, suggested Giacomoni, who had first introduced stretch materials in the Versace lines. Yes, said Donatella, "and also leggings and many kinds of accessories. Gianni creates the clothes and I combine them with shoes and bags and jewelry that make them look modern. I want them modern, and I'll criticize certain things Gianni designs just as I'll criticize the dresses on Allegra's dolls if they have too many *volants*. By now Allegra is always asking me: do you think this looks modern? But beyond modernity, one thing I'm absolutely convinced of is that you must have fun when you work in fashion."

While Gianni was supervising the rehearsal, correcting the models, calling for the indispensible Franca Biagini, the head fitter, dealing with the filming of the TV special with Karl Lagerfeld that would air a few days later, he was also talking to a couple of journalists, expressing the doubts that perennially assailed him before the clothes went out on the runway: "How will it go, this show? Too classic? Too modern? It's not that I don't know how to make them, the kind of clothes that everyone here in Paris makes. It just seems pointless to me to show them. They are like a song we've already heard." Using the Ritz's covered pool as his runway, to the beat of *The Most Beautiful Girl in the World*, Versace sent out galactic minidresses in space colors, wrote Suzy Menkes in the *International Herald Tribune* under the headline, "Versace's Cyberspace Couture." The glamorous models in glittering colored dresses of computer-programmed chain mail drew applause from the likes of Sylvester Stallone, Prince, Roman Polanski, Emmanuelle Seigner, Vincent Perez, and the millionaire magician David Copperfield, Claudia Schiffer's boyfriend at the time. Then came the sheepskin jackets all the more beguiling in their colors of mother-of-pearl, rose, lilac and sky blue. There was also a "snakeskin" dress, for which Versace had taken nappa leather and treated it with thermofusion techniques to give it a shiny, scaly effect that even felt like snakeskin. And also handsome dinner jackets for evening wear, brightly colored and cut to show cleavage, to wear over miniskirts made of tiny squares of harlequin-colored, fluorescent patent leather.

When the show was over, Donatella celebrated her ten years of work as chief of the Versace image with her supermodel friends at the Ritz disco. Music by Prince to entertain 400 guests: all could watch and dance with Cindy Crawford, Carla Bruni, Christy Turlington, Linda Evangelista, the young Brandy and others. Donatella was feeling proud of them. "I know them and I know how to take them," she told *Corriere della Sera*. "I know their assets and their defects." And she had a nice word to say about all of them. Carla Bruni? "She's cultivated, a nice person. She doesn't talk like a model and she has one of the most beautiful bodies ever seen." Claudia Schiffer? "I was struck right away by her extraordinary beauty. And yet she was terribly unsure of herself and she walked badly. And it's true, she's very modest. Only Avedon could have photographed her as Eve," Donatella added, referring to that winter's ad campaign for Versace in which Schiffer appeared wearing only a Home Collection duvet, a photo session for which she was paid a record $30,000. Linda Evangelista? "She's considered the most difficult. She always has something to say—about the clothes, about the photographer's lights—and she's the most snobby and the laziest. But with me, she behaves herself." And Naomi Campbell, with her reputation as rebellious and dislikable? "She doesn't have a good reputation, no, but I adore her. It's true, she has a temper, but with me she's well-behaved and even a bit jealous of me. When she walks down the runway she's a panther, she can devour the world. She has tender, delicate skin. She's the only black model to make the covers of *Vogue*, *Harper's Bazaar* and even *Time*. She eats a lot and pretty badly. She's chaotic in her love life, too—from De Niro to Clapton."

When the Paris shows were over, things turned sour for Gianni Versace. He fell ill. On his return from a visit to America, he found he had lost his hearing in one ear. He didn't worry about it at first, thinking he would resolve the problem with a visit to the ear, nose and throat doctor to have his ear canal washed out. But then his cheek swelled up. He needed further exams, which were carried out at the San Raffaele hospital in Milan. The diagnosis was not the most heartening. Santo Versace talked about it in a December 2006 interview in the Italian monthly *Business People*. " Between August 1994 and October 1995 Gianni had chemotherapy," he recalls. "He feared he might not make it after they found he had a cancer of the ear. And that was when he began to let Donatella take over part of the creative work. He said to me, 'Santo, you have to tell me what you think Gianni Versace S.p.A. will be after my death. I know what it will be as long as I'm here. But we must begin to think about afterwards.' The chemotherapy went well and by the end of 1995 Gianni was back on the job, more determined than ever."

During his treatment, Versace slowed his work rhythm, relying on the affectionate assistance of his colleagues. He slept a bit in the afternoon and took an extra day on the weekends at his " Proustian" residence on Lake Como, where he felt protected and reassured. Gigi Scagliotti, an architect, great friend and Gianni's companion on many, many trips around the world—from Turkey to Vietnam, from the Algerian desert to Polynesia, on long voyages in the Americas, like that from Colorado to Cabo San Lucas—has a particular memory of that period. "I went to see Gianni in Miami in the summer of 1994, when he wasn't feeling well, and Donatella, Allegra and Antonio were there with him. We used to go and skate out front of his house on Ocean Drive. Our days went more or less like this: in the morning we all had breakfast with Gianni at home, and then around nine a.m. I used to go with him to the usual café where he would buy armfuls of newspapers and magazines. We'd go back home. He would close himself up in his studio with Donatella to talk about fashion and clothes and the rest of us would go to the beach. In the evening we'd go out to dinner; we often went to eat Japanese food. Gianni would go to bed early, while Donatella, Antonio and Michel and I would go to the disco. Gianni didn't go out much; he used to get tired. But we never talked about illness. I had the impression there in Miami that he was putting a lot of responsibility on Donatella, but I wouldn't go so far as to say he thought he was going to die. A year later he felt better and then he was back in great form again and he took the reins back in hand. Donatella was always of the utmost importance for him. Their relationship was one of great affection and complicity, but there was also conflict. They used to fight a lot, in dialect so that no one could understand them, and her mascara used to run down her face. It was after his illness, in the shows of the last years, that Gianni began to come out on the runway with Donatella."

On September 15 Versace would once again be hosted by an important museum. The Kunstgewerbemuseum in Berlin put on his show "Gianni Versace Signature" in a new version that would run through the end of November. Divided into six sections—embroidery, timeless clothes, prints, leather, theater costumes and the home—the exhibit was a hymn to a virtuoso talent that astonished the Germans and conquered whole pages in the newspapers. Unfortunately Versace, who was thrilled by his reception in this new capital of a newly unified Germany, got a little carried away in his comments, which reflected a tense moment in Italian politics. "There are times when I'm ashamed to call myself an Italian. When it comes to fashion, our politicians deserve a big F. We have to keep going forward, but pretty soon it looks like they'll be putting even saints through the Inquisition.... I'd like to see more culture in the city where I live, and more respect for fashion, which is also culture."

The next day his outburst was featured in all of Italy's dailies. And Gianni was annoyed. He insisted he had many kind words to say about Italian culture—the culture out of which his work had emerged, after all—during the press conference for the opening of the Berlin exhibit. Somewhat bitter, he withdrew to make the last adjustments to his collections and to cultivate Madonna on the phone (he had met her in Miami and she had promised to attend his fashion show) in hopes she would do as she said. Madonna had gotten bored with backing the young designers Dolce & Gabbana and had suddenly gone crazy about Versace haute couture.

Meanwhile Santo Versace, on the list of those under investigation in the Clean Hands corruption inquiry, had been summoned by the public prosecutor Antonio Di Pietro to his office on the fourth floor of Milan's courthouse. As the chairman and CEO of Gianni Versace S.p.A. Santo stood accused of having paid millions of lire in bribes to earn the indulgence of the tax and customs police each time they came to inspect the company's books. The company was not the only one under investigation among the fashion designers. There were also Armani (who resolved his case with a plea bargain), Krizia, Ferré, Etro and Basile. Along with the others, Versace would eventually be acquitted in the Cassation Court, the top appeals court, "for not having committed the crime."

In October all these troubles, both judicial and not, melted away like snow on a sunny day. The fashion shows for the spring-summer 1995 collections were simply outstanding. The watchword among all the designers, Armani included, was to amaze—and not to worry about overdoing it. In this regard, Versace had been ahead of his time, as Natalia Aspesi pointed out in *la Repubblica.* "He sniffed the atmosphere well ahead of all the others, and that explains his ever-more diabolical success. His hyper-women, with their hyper-bosoms and their hyper-bottoms, need hyper-garments for a hyper-life that he alone is capable of depicting, and with a lot more glitz than the others. The basic item for next summer's wardrobes is going to be the Versace bodice out of which spring a pair of sassy, S&M-TV breasts." On the runway, Versace's supermodels looked like a perfect cross between Barbie and Marilyn Monroe, sexy and come-hither, squeezed into their plastic-look bustiers and their lacquered miniskirts in gold and silver, but also able to wear pastel suits in blue, dusty rose and lilac checks decorated with butterflies and ladybugs. It was this second aspect of the show that Suzy Menkes, writing in the *International Herald Tribune,* referred to in an article headlined, "Versace: Rare Understatement," in which she also applauded his long dresses with leg-revealing slits. And as always, the show offered an audience full of celebrities, including Elton John and Sylvester Stallone, to thrill the crowds piled up on the sidewalks outside Via Gesù.

The following month, Versace published *L'uomo senza cravatta* with Leonardo Arte, a 274-page celebration of male beauty drawing on the advertising photos done by Avedon, Weber and Ritts. Among the sculptured nudes, there were also portraits of Versace, who wrote in the book's afterword, "My first idea was to do a book on men's fashions. But when I came to select the drawings and photos from the archives, I realized that all these years I had been dealing with people whom I considered to be free from any kind of constriction. That's it, that's what I believe in, and this is a book about my style."

As the year drew to a close, there was a growing malaise in the world of fashion. Sociologist Francesco Alberoni, in one of his opinion pieces in *Corriere della Sera*, put it pretty clearly: "Italian style now has a new enemy: envy." The envious were those Italian politicians who looked down on home-grown fashion, on the French labels and also the Americans. And now Versace found himself the target of two English-language publications: *The Independent* suggested in an article of its Sunday supplement that the balance sheets of Gianni Versace S.p.A. were not very transparent, and alleged the company had links to the Mafia. And Gianni thought *The New Yorker*, a magazine that he adored, gave too little space to Italian designers like him, Armani and Valentino, when it dealt with fashion—even when the editors commissioned big names like John Updike and Salman Rushdie to write about it. Santo responded to the first criticism, citing numbers and sales and announcing new stores soon to open in England. And Gianni reacted to *The New Yorker*'s neglect in an article in *Corriere della Sera*. "I've distanced myself from things. Today I want to communicate solely through my work, the horizons of which are expanding. I'm referring to the clothes first of all, but also to the things for the home, to my work for the cinema, the ballet and the theater. And also my involvement in the world of rock music and photography. Because fashion isn't everything."

CHAPTER 17
Lady Di

Nude men on megascreens decorated the runway for the fall-winter 1995–1996 collections: Versace's look for the new year was bold, brazen and provocative. That year, the Versace man wore pin-striped jackets that fell to the knees, V-necked sweaters with optical designs, perfect blazers and tailored dinner jackets. A few days after his show, Versace sponsored one of the most beautiful photography exhibits ever seen in Milan, a huge retrospective of the work of Richard Avedon that came from the Whitney Museum in New York, mounted under Avedon's supervision in the Sala dei Cariatidi at Palazzo Reale. The show consisted of 600 black-and-white prints that documented Avedon's fifty years of work. Divided into three sections, the first included work for Gianni Versace, who had sought out Avedon for his ad campaigns right from the start. The second section was made up of work done for various fashion magazines. The third and most striking section was dedicated to Avedon's reportage—his famous sequences on psychiatric hospitals among the mentally ill, his shots of the suburbs of Palermo and New York, his shocking documentation of napalm-bomb victims in Vietnam and finally, his portraits of his dying father. The Versace family chose the occasion to offer to head up a possible campaign to restore Palazzo Reale, Milan's largest exhibition space, having just a few months before sponsored the restoration and reopening of Milan's Palazzo Bagatti Valsecchi.

In Paris, Versace led off the haute couture fashion shows with his Atelier collection. The atmosphere had changed for everyone. The too-sexy, too-naked look seemed to have come to the end of its cycle. John Fairchild spoke of a new trend, "conservative chic." The designers acquiesced, even Versace. Although he continued to cherish his statuesque supermodels, he now dressed them in haute couture style, with a nod at the great artisans of elegance—Vionnet, Balenciaga, Dior. And he softened the appeal with pastel colors. He told Laura Laurenzi of *la Repubblica*, "I think we've galloped through the century, from the Belle Epoque to today. Now we're heading toward the end of the millennium, and everything is going to change. We'll move toward a further simplification. Meanwhile I've given couture a facelift using minimalist details." Sitting in the front row, Valentino attended a Versace show for the first time. He applauded and came backstage to congratulate Versace. "Very Versace," he said, "and so full of energy." Writing in *Le Figaro*, Jamie Samet noted that Versace's "James Bond girls" had earned a star for good conduct, for being demure women of the "wife" category "with their little white gloves, their *pochettes*, the ribbons in their hair, their straight skirts down below the knee under jackets buttoned up to the neck."

And if even Madonna, putting the hard eros of *Sex* and the thriller *Body of Evidence* behind her, could go for the new wave Gianni Versace couture, it must mean something. Madonna is the sort of star who's adept at changing her style when the social winds of fashion change. Having bid a friendly farewell to Dolce & Gabbana, Madonna moved over to become the protagonist of Versace's new ad campaign photographed by Steven Meisel. In it she would appear as a sexy, but also romantic and chic, woman wearing a pastel-colored suit under the bright Palm Beach sun. By her side, there was a baby carriage, and two babies were naked on the grass— as it happens, the lawn of Donald Trump's estate at Mar-a-Lago.

"Gianni Versce's advertising campaigns were real Hollywood-style productions," says Andrea Tremolada, who was in charge of publicity for Versace between 1994 and 2006. "There were never less than forty or fifty people on the set. Gianni wanted advertising inserts in all the world's most important magazines, an incredible number of pages with respect to the budget at hand. On average we were running 2,500 advertising pages a year between fashion, accessories and fragrances, from the multiple pages we ran in *Vogue* America or *Rolling Stone*, to single pages in *The New Yorker* or *Interview*. Gianni had a big book, a sort of chess board on which we plotted the names of the publications and the months in which the ads would run. He would choose different images for each publication and he invariably changed each one two or three times before they came out. He supervised everything; if he found out that a substitution hadn't been made, he'd be furious. And there would be hell to pay if you didn't go to the printer to check the quality of the photographs. And this would happen even when he was in Miami or was traveling; he'd call up at three or four a.m. to reach us while we were in the office and tell us to go get the fax he had just sent and read it right away. He was a galvanizer—he put a huge amount of energy into every aspect of his work and he transmitted that energy to all of us."

After the Paris shows, Versace's conservative chic was so *in* that when the Council of Fashion Designers of America convened in New York at the end of January to hand out its Oscars for fashion, Princess Diana was invited. And she asked Versace to make her a dress for the party ($1,000 a head to participate). It wasn't the first Versace gown Diana had worn; the first was in 1992, just after her separation from Prince Charles, when he refused to end his liaison with the determined Camilla Parker-Bowles. And "that long, form-fitting dress of pale blue satin with its glistening gold embroidery, that revealed her blue-blooded young bosom," wrote Natalia Aspesi in *la Repubblica*, "transformed the pretty princess with her frightened air into a beautiful young woman of fearless, almost brazen style. In other words, a Versace woman."

Lady Di's switch to Versace's fashion, so different from the stuffy and institutional style of Bruce Oldfield, Queen Elizabeth's dressmaker, who was imposed on Diana in the early years of her marriage, was part of a well-thought-out plan to change her image. Diana wanted to—she felt she must—become a different woman. She surrounded herself with experts from various disciplines. One of them was Peter Settelen, who helped her change the way she presented herself and spoke. He explained it to Monica Bogliardi of *Panorama*: "She spoke in short phrases, her breathing was poor, she was tense. I taught her how to make her breathing more fluid and how to dissolve the tension that accumulates at the center of the torso. With a year's work, I was able to bring out her natural voice, which was deep, calm, and sexy."

That voice would glue 200 million viewers to their TV sets on November 20, to watch the famous BBC interview. A few days later, a *Daily Telegraph* poll revealed Princess Diana's stunning popularity, and *Time* put her on its cover. And not only did Diana benefit from the services of her media coach, she also profited from the help of psychologists, particularly the feminist psychotherapist Susie Orbach, who helped the princess repair her damaged self-esteem, which had pushed her into bulimia. Ann Harvey, deputy editor of British *Vogue*, also helped Diana modify her look, suggesting she wear clothes by Versace and Lacroix. Diana, now slim and beautiful, more sure of herself and elegantly sexy, became an icon. Versace sent his Atelier haute couture collections to the princess at her residence, Kensington Palace, so that she could choose the items she liked. Once she had chosen, Versace, who had a mannequin with Diana's measurements in Via Gesù, would send his head fitter Franca Biagini along with two seamstresses to adjust the clothes to perfection. Among Diana's many public appearances wearing Versace, there was her unforgettable visit to Mother Teresa of Calcutta, when she wore dresses with slightly scooped necklines and matching jackets, very simple and very couture.

Versace admired that "star quality" in her that won over the crowds, but also her human qualities, her informality and ability to be genuine and candid. Apropos of those qualities, Antonio D'Amico recalls the time that "Gianni and I were guests for the weekend of Elton and David[1] in their estate near Windsor—the house had once belonged to Queen Elizabeth's personal physician. On Saturday night Elton invited some people for dinner, among them Diana, Hugh Grant and Elizabeth Hurley. Diana came by car from London, alone. Elton, who is very entertaining, dominated the dinner table conversation, talking about what was happening in London, the latest gossip in the fashion and show business worlds. It was a jolly evening. When it came time for coffee, we moved into the sitting room with the fireplace. Gradually, the conversation turned more intimate. Diana, along with Elizabeth, was perched on the carpet in front of the seating area. She was relaxed, she was laughing and enjoying the evening. She talked about Charles, about how she loved him and would have done anything to keep him by her side. We all talked about ourselves, as one does among friends. When we went up to bed, Gianni commented that it was a real shame that a woman as tender and as beautiful as Diana should feel alone and deceived, that she did not have a true love."

---

1. David Furnish, Elton John's partner.

Back in Milan in March, Versace sent out his fall-winter collection 1995–1996, a collection that followed the conservative chic glamour he had showed with Atelier in Paris. There were suits with form-fitting skirts, slinky stretch sheaths, coats for career women that looked perfectly sewed-on and dazzling evening dresses in satin and chiffon received with cheers and burst of applause. "I wanted to dress busy women, women who work hard in their careers and who understand the secret equilibrium between decorum, refinement and the power to enchant," Versace told *la Repubblica*. "The new look for next winter could be called 'day-time glamour.' It's designed to help a woman keep her womanliness in mind always, so that she provokes admiration and a certain awe while discouraging any unwanted sexual advances."

Versace had just won his lawsuit against the British daily *The Independent* for the ferocious article in its Sunday supplement that cast doubt on the truth of the company's accounts. The newspaper had to print an apology and pay him £100,000. The designer took the opportunity to send out a press release with all the details of his company's rise and current success. "In 1983 we had sales of 250 billion lire, and ten years later the Versace brand has sales of over 1 trillion lire. There are 138 Versace boutiques around the world and 340 sales points, not to mention our second lines, which are sold in 2,659 stores. We employ 800 people and give jobs to another 5,000," he informed the press. He also announced that he was "pleased to have bought a building on Central Park in New York for the whole family: my brother Santo, my sister Donatella and my nieces and nephews. I've also taken a thirty-year lease on Vanderbilt House, built in 1902 by the Hunt Brothers—a Louis XV-style jewel and now my favorite. Its five floors and 2,850 square meters of floor space will be our new boutique."

America liked his new demure luxury. *Time* put a splendid Claudia Schiffer on its cover wearing a cream-colored Versace suit that was the standard-bearer of the new trend, over the title "Simply Beautiful." A six-page cover story talked about how fashion had returned to the classics. For Versace, it was a genuine consecration. The U.S. weekly had devoted few of its covers to fashion over the years. There was Elsa Schiaparelli in 1932; then Pierre Cardin had his turn. Then there was Brooke Shields modeling for Valentino in 1981, and Giorgio Armani in 1982. And now it was Versace's turn, as the designer, trimming and pruning, opened the way to a new elegance that was inspired, so he himself explained, by Katharine Hepburn and Grace Kelly. Versace, who couldn't have been happier about the *Time* cover, had this to say: "The time is right for well-made clothes. And the time is right for Italy, which is enjoying an amazing success in America. My sales in the U.S. have grown 40 percent. All the actresses want my clothes. After Madonna, who posed for my most recent ad campaign, a lot of singers want to be photographed in my clothes, too. Tomorrow it will be Prince's turn; he'll be photographed by Avedon. Later this week it will be Michael Jackson." Meanwhile Sylvester Stallone had called up to ask Versace to make a wedding dress for Angie Everhart, whom he was planning to marry. Even Miami awarded Versace a prize: the Florida Trust for Historical Preservation presented him with a award for his restoration work on Casa Casuarina.

But at that moment, Gianni was in love with New York. In May, he bought a house in the heart of Manhattan, on one of the most desirable streets of the Upper East Side, 64th Street, very near the townhouses belonging to Ivana Trump, David Geffen, Pierre Cardin and Donna Summer. It cost him $7.5 million. Proud of this latest sumptuous purchase, Versace told *The New York Observer*: "I've asked Philip Taaffe to take care of the library, Julian Schnabel to paint the bedroom, and Roy Lichtenstein to provide the paintings for the entry hall." For several years Versace had been a fan of contemporary art. "Gianni met Julian Schnabel through Elton John," explained Wanda Galtrucco. "I remember very well the first time we went to see Schnabel in his studio downtown, a big loft with very high ceilings that had been an old brewery. We stayed quite a while, because Gianni liked to develop a personal relationship with the artists. He did the same with Bob Rauschenberg, Roy Lichtenstein, Jeff Koons and Jim Dine. Gianni bought many works from each of them, following the advice of Larry Gagosian, the hippest, most exclusive contemporary art dealer in New York. In turn Gianni took many ideas from these artists and borrowed them for his clothes, from Andy Warhol's Marilyn Monroe to Jim Dine's hearts."

For Gianni, the New York house represented

modernity, a world that was moving forward, moving fast. When the *Observer* asked him on what basis he had chosen his various homes, he replied they all represented "a sense of continuity. All my houses have a past: the Milan house was a convent, while the villa on Lake Como belonged to a nudist from London in the 18th century. And this house in New York belonged to a woman who loved Italy: when I came in and saw her old Ferragamo shoes and her collections of *Vogue Italia*, I immediately felt at ease."

At the end of June, Versace sent out his spring-summer menswear collection at Via Gesù in Milan. This time the Versace man was a man of the future, sporting techno-fabrics inspired by what the NASA astronauts wore. Water-repellant jackets and rubberized pants, velcro and hooks and eyes instead of buttons all gave an attractive spin to his Gianni Versace collection and to the Versus and Istante lines. All offered a preview, in terms of the materials and how they were worked, of some of the themes he would introduce with Atelier in Paris in July.

But first, he was off to a party in London, where he was looking to buy another house. It was a huge celebrity event at Emporium, his store on Old Bond Street, to raise funds for Elton John's AIDS Foundation. The occasion was the publication of the English language edition of *Men Without Ties*, with its cover shot of a handsome Marcus Schenkenberg posing nude. Gianni, who usually wore a black cashmere-and-silk sweater, dressed that night in a white turtleneck to greet his guests. Seven hundred had been invited, among them Bob Geldof and

Michael Caine, Greta Scacchi and Zucchero, Rod Stewart and Jerry Hall, George Michael and Pierce Brosnan, the painter Sebastian Matta, Trudy Styler without her husband Sting and of course all his favorite supermodels, from Naomi Campbell to Kate Moss. Amid the rose petals sprinkled over the tables, the bottles of Krug champagne and the platters of lobster and oysters, £100,000 in AIDS funds were pledged. Princess Diana, who had promised to appear at the party, had second thoughts and did not show up. But she made it up to "fabulous Gianni," as he was called there, with an invitation to lunch at Kensington Palace.

Just a few days later he was in Paris for the haute couture shows. At three p.m. in the Place Vendôme in front of the Ritz, the crowd outside Versace's show included not only the usual photographers and fans but also a crowd of kids waiting to catch a glimpse of Madonna. After her starring role in Versace's new ad campaign, the singer was seated in the front row next to her Cuban companion Carlos Leon. There was also Prince, who offered the forty-five minutes of music to accompany the show, as well as Meg Ryan, Rupert Everett, Charlotte Rampling and Bryan Ferry. When Gianni's magnificent supermodels strode out on the runway, all the clothes they wore were white—the supershort miniskirts, the bodices closed with rhinestone-covered zippers, the overcoats with their *carré* pattern, the boots reminiscent of Courrèges and the seventies, the cellophane crinolines and the pearly sheath of a wedding dress with an embroidered denim veil. "The revolution has begun in haute couture," wrote Janie Samet in *Le Figaro*. While he was in Paris, Versace was interviewed by the American gay publication *The Advocate*, which pressed him for his views on the role of gays in the fashion world. "I've been this way for 47 years," Versace said, "and I'm at ease with myself, I'm happy." He said the same in an interview with *The New York Times* in which he made his relationship with Antonio D'Amico official. A few months later he would tell Alessandra Farkas of *Corriere della Sera*, "My friends and those who love me know very well that I am gay. Why shout it with a megaphone?" The reporter continued to pursue the matter, noting that "some of those friends, from Elton John to K.D. Lang, have made their homosexuality into a rallying cry...." And Versace replied: "We ought to imitate them in Italy, too, but unfortunately our society is very different, it obliges you to hide your private life. American gays are a highly respected political and economic force. Our problem is that we have the Vatican here in our own backyard. If the Vatican were elsewhere, we'd be free. Instead, we're surrounded by an obsession about sin. We're judged, catalogued and stifled by a castrating upbringing."

In that tumultuous year of 1995, Versace opened a sumptuous new store in Milan, buying the old Palazzo Ricordi on Via Montenapoleone 2, which Magnoli and Carmellini would rehab and redecorate in grand style, with plaster moldings, marble, columns and mosaics. When the store was sold in 1999, rumor would had it that Vuitton paid 30 billion lire to take over the building.

On October 9 at the Milan fashion shows for spring-summer 1996, Versace earned the most convinced acclaim he had ever garnered in his whole career. Buyers and fashion editors alike loved his glamorous, pared-down chemisiers, with their clean lines and play of transparency over the back and décolleté. Princess Diana had already ordered several in different colors and by way of thanks, Versace dedicated to her the handbag with the Medusas that she held when *Paris Match* photographed her. Versace also offered new suits with clever cuts, little fabric belts, new lengths for tops that uncovered the navel, skirts revved up with pleats and godets, slightly draped evening gowns and gowns with skirts of transparent black chiffon. If it all looked simple, it was the kind of simplicity that only a great couturier knows how to pull off. The hard-to-please Suzy Menkes wrote about "skinny rib sweaters" and "A-line skirts" that were "cute."

The Gianni Versace group remained in excellent form. The financial press, reviewing the balance sheets of the fashion business, once again ranked Versace beside Armani, who was still in first place. "As 1994 comes to an end, our direct and indirect sales are worth 1.22 trillion lire, up 20 percent on last year's performance," Santo Versace announced. "And we expect the same growth this year. From 1990 we've been investing some 40 billion lire a year to open new sales points all around the world." In 1995, there were 225 Versace boutiques around the world and sales points had risen to 3,000.

Just now Versace was looking across the Atlantic. On October 28, when fashion week opened in New York, the first show would be that of Versus, designed by Donatella, the guiding spirit behind this youthful collection. This would be her international debut. "My sister's strength? She makes everything she touches modern," Gianni told *Panorama*. There were huge crowds for the show at Bryant Park, and giant balloons over the Hudson River advertising Versus. Nobody wanted to miss Versace's "Good Girls and Bad Girls" as the press called them: they were sporting little white skirts, fluorescent shirtwaists, synthetic fabrics and street-look camisoles, boots and opaque stockings. And nobody wanted to miss the after-show party at Twilo, where 2,000 guests were invited, among them Donald Trump, Kate Moss, Naomi Campbell and Lou Reed.

Back in Milan the following month, Versace presented his new book, *Do Not Disturb*, published by Leonardo Arte, a coffee table volume devoted to his various glamorous homes. The photos of Villa Fontanelle at Moltrasio on Lake Como, of his Milanese residence and of Casa Casuarina in Miami had been taken by Avedon, Weber and Newton, who over the years had recorded his several houses and shot portraits in them of Versace's family and close friends. "The only hobby I have is my houses," Versace told the press. "They are the places where I go to be by myself. I like to read and isolate myself from the world. Then I emerge from my mental oasis to design clothes and home fashions that are all the more more alive and transgressive. What's my favorite house? Moltrasio. In Milan, there's work; Miami is the place dedicated to my friends, to socializing. At Villa Fontanelle, on the other hand, I get my soul back. I put my slippers on and make space for my memories. The villa is where I can say that I am truly at home."

The year ended on a high note. On December 3, Gianni was in New York to receive a prize for "most innovative designer with the greatest influence on music" from the MTV Fashion in Music Awards. Madonna and Elton John handed him the prize before a crowd of celebrities. There would be another party the following night, when the exhibit *Haute Couture* opened at the Metropolitan Museum of Art. Sponsored by Versace and Chanel and curated by Richard Martin and Harold Koda, the show reviewed the highlights of high fashion from the Second Empire to contemporary times. Only two Italians were included: Versace and Valentino. "It's tremendously thrilling," Versace wrote in a comment in *la Repubblica*. "In haute couture we see all the ability and the learning of those who know how to put their hands to best use. Agile, clever hands that can stitch exquisite embroideries, weave delicate threads into fabrics, execute a perfect row of cross-stitch. And there is more. Haute couture is the only art that changes when it accomodates new technologies, yet always remains the same."

CHAPTER 18
Manhattan

Even fashionistas, the sort of people so cool that novelty doesn't faze them, were taken aback by the invitation to Versace's menswear show at the beginning of 1996. The photo, courtesy of Avedon, showed a male nude sporting, between his legs, deliciously feminine attributes. It was another Versace-style punch in the stomach. But it also said a lot about how intensely fashion was now striving to grab attention, to rekindle the interest of the public. There was an almost desperate need to make every fashion event more spectacular, more newsworthy, and to that end more and more celebrities were being brought in as models and to pad the rows of guests. At Versace's show the hottest guest of 1996 was Robbie Williams, ex-leader of Take That, who, arriving at Via Gesù around six p.m. provoked a traffic jam that spread all the way to the cross street Via Montenapoleone, due to the huge mob of his fans. Versace sent out military-look uniforms with feminine touches and jackets in animal hide prints, but also perfect dresses matched with long, narrow jackets that had thin, raised lapels. About the Versus show, Suzy Menkes in the *The New York Times*, wrote of "the ultra-hip Versus line from Gianni Versace (blue nail polish an optional accessory)."

In Paris, haute couture was looking a bit thin. Names like Cardin, Lanvin and Carven had disappeared from the calendar. *Le Monde* ran a long article by Laurence Benaïm suggesting that couturiers were paralyzed by tax rules, lacked points of reference and were suffering an all-out identity crisis. "Haute Couture, a Splendid Twilight," the French daily warned. Only a few solid French fashion houses weren't concerned about the crisis: Chanel, guided by Lagerfeld; Dior, with Ferré at its head; Givenchy, in the hands of the young Englishman John Galliano; and Lacroix. Thus the Italians who showed their collections in Paris—Versace and Valentino—were particularly well liked in France. And in fact each was recognized by the Paris Chamber of Fashion as a *"membre correspondant"*— that is to say, as an official guest on the Paris fashion show calendar.

Versace did not let Paris down. He brought out an ultra-sexy collection, backed up by original music composed by Elton John and donated to his friend Gianni. The forty-five minute show at the Ritz was a stunning spectacle of transparent lacy lingerie-look vests matched with leather or metal mesh, and underneath, the clearly visible outlines of dazzling haute couture underpants. There were also abbreviated coats and short dresses to the knee in optical-look patterns with black-and-white lines, as well as zebra-stripe and leopard-spot patterns. Janie Samet, writing in *Le Figaro*, said, "Gianni Versace swears he has never before done something so simple. What a shameless liar! You have to have all his cleverness to make women into objects of permanent desire without once descending into vulgarity." Only Pierre Bergé, chairman of Saint Laurent, had a nasty word to say. He accused haute couture (and thus his own partner Yves Saint Laurent) of being obsolete, "because life no longer consists of balls and evenings at the opera," and he mentioned Versace in particular, who in turn replied that he couldn't care less about Bergé's opinion, given that even *The New York Times* had good things to say about his Atelier collection.

Meanwhile, Gianni was looking East. Versace was one of just a few Italian designers (including Valentino, Zegna, Ferragamo and Fendi) who had already opened stores and sales points in major Chinese cities. He had begun in 1993 with two boutiques at the Seibu department store in Shenzhen in the textile-producing province of Guangdong. And now he had opened his first shops in Beijing and Shanghai, with plans to open more before July. "The location of our boutiques is of the utmost importance," Santo Versace told *Il Sole 24 Ore*. "We want our image in China to be right for a luxury goods group, and therefore we're looking only at top luxury hotels and exclusive shopping centers. Our impression is that the Chinese client likes clothes and products that are highly innovative. In particular, the Gianni Versace womenswear collection, our handbags, neckties and accessories in general are doing very well. We expect our sales this year to reach 25 billion lire. And for the next three years, the forecast is for growth of 35 percent per year."

As the prêt-à-porter shows in March approached, the usual race to find celebrities to invite (often at a cost of several million lire) had begun. Versace, who was the first to understand the benefits of spectacularizing fashion—and who did so amply—now lowered his tone and handpicked the guests for his show. In the first row, along with Prince, would be Woody Allen, who was on tour playing jazz clarinet in Milan, and who would join Gianni for lunch at Via Gesù, with Soon-Yi Previn and Allen's cinematographer Carlo Di Palma and his wife, Adriana. "I feel I've known you all my life," Versace recalled that the great director told him.

But this time it was fashion that grabbed the headlines—Versace's fashion. The fall-winter collection that appeared on his runway was both elegant and practical: a chic sport-look that was also glamorous, it included dresses that fell straight from the shoulders cinched with tiny belts, in colors of fuchsia, lilac and pale blue, to wear with cardigans knotted at the waist, short coats in pale colors, leather pants matched with black chiffon shirts, chain mail miniskirts decorated with rhinestones, petite lacquered cashmere sweaters, and naturally, Versace's evergreen style for evening—lingerie-look long dresses, in two colors or with lace inserts. The audience was ecstatic. And Soon-Yi Previn, soon to be Mrs. Woody Allen, was so taken that the next day she spent two hours shopping in the Via Montenapoleone boutique.

"I was aiming at chic minimalism, at avant-garde conservatism," Versace commented on the show. And he seemed to have succeeded in finding the right balance. At Prada—which according to *Women's Wear Daily's* John

Fairchild did not succeed—Miuccia Prada had gone so far as to close her doors to the Italian daily press, which according to her, tended to dedicate too much space to celebrities and not enough to fashion.

And at the end of March, Gianni and Donatella racked up another success with the Versus line, presented for the second year at Bryant Park in New York (the show was also projected live on a mega-screen in Times Square). Among the guests were Bianca Jagger, Mike Tyson, Lisa Marie Presley and once again Woody Allen, who, it was rumored, was interested in fashion because he contemplated making a film about the fashion world. The resounding applause confirmed that this younger Versace line—slender coats to mid-calf, chiffon dresses with asymmetrical necklines, African-style graphic prints, long silk jersey evening dresses—pleased American tastes. The numbers backed that up, for Versus's total sales the previous year had amounted to 140 billion lire, of which 37 percent were U.S. sales, while the mere appearance of Versus at the previous year's New York fashion week had boosted sales world-wide by 35 percent.

Meanwhile over at Saks, Donatella was introducing her new fragrance, Blonde. In just five days Blonde would rack up $170,000 in sales at the company's forty-five U.S. sales points. The Versace siblings' stay in New York concluded with an evening at Versace's home on East 64th Street to watch Oscar night in Los Angeles on TV. Gianni, who was responsible for the Oscar night fashions of Anjelica Huston, Elton John and John Travolta, had installed a big screen on one wall of the "garden" room on the ground floor, a room decorated with the dream-like floral murals of Frank Moore. He invited some thirty people to watch the show, among them Moore himself, Julian Schnabel, K.D. Lang and a small group of journalists including Ingrid Sischy, the editor of *Interview*. For once Gianni, who didn't like to stay awake late, enjoyed being up after midnight.

It made sense that America should figure ever-larger in Versace's balance sheets. In addition to the investment in Versus, there was the new mega-store on Fifth Avenue and the new offices about to open in a Manhattan high rise. But for Versace, as for other fashion houses, clothing sales were declining with respect to other group products. Santo Versace, interviewed by Mario Platero of *Il Sole 24 Ore*, explained that "from the current level of 60 percent they will fall to 33 percent inside the year 2000. The outlook for 1996 is good: we expect indirect sales to reach 1.5 trillion lire and to see direct sales of 650 billion lire. The Italian market represents about 20 percent of the total. The variation in the percentage of group sales from clothing is explained by the expansion of those sectors that Gianni Versace believes can grow even more rapidly. Ranking those sectors in order of importance, we have: first, perfumes and fragrances [in 1994 Versace had taken control of Giver, the company that produces and sells his fragrances], a sector that is expected to grow from the current 145 billion lire in sales to 500 billion lire worth over the next three years. Then we have items for the home, where our three-year goal is to move from the expected 1996 sales of 100 billion lire to 400 million lire worth.

Accessories, presently worth 200 billion lire in sales, should rise to 400 billion lire worth in the next three years. Jewelry and timepieces should expand from the current 50 billion lire in sales to some 300 billion lire worth."

Princess Diana, meanwhile, continued to be Versace's most formidable celebrity clothes horse. In Chicago, where she was attending a society ball at the Museum of Natural History to raise funds for cancer research, she appeared in a Versace gown. The crowd behind police lines was waiting only for her—and when she arrived, people erupted in delirium. On August 27 in New York, Versace opened the doors to his newest boutique at 647 Fifth Avenue near 52nd Street in the former Vanderbilt house, an early 20th-century building lovingly restored by Versace's architects using a supply of the original Vermont marble from an out-of-commission quarry, traced to a stockpile in Carrara back in Italy. In restoring the five-story building of marble and glass, the biggest Versace store in the world, the designer focused more on the architecture than on the decoration, and the store was given a strong contemporary feel with prominent artworks like Peter Schuyff's American flag, and illumination by lighting designer David Schemmer. *The New York Times* gave its benediction to Versace's new showcase, which cost the company some $32 million, writing that, "with its vermiculated ('worm-eaten') marble facade and fluted Corinthian columns, restored, the townhouse is resplendent."

Versace, who as always worked with architects Magnoli and Carmellini, explained he wanted to use the new store to change the way he offered his clothes to the public. "The idea is to put the collections on display," he told *Panorama*. "Not just those presented on the runway, but special collections, beginning with evening clothes. Shoppers who come in here will find not only what was shown in Paris or in Milan, but haute couture clothing and models linked to the latest trends. Today, newspapers and the media exhaust the new quickly. In order to evolve, one has to find new ways of communicating one's personal style, and in market terms, to get the products to consumers in the most direct way. This is the future: not just two collections, or rather four, counting the two Atelier collections, but also another two. In short, there will be six Versace collections. That way I can refresh the ideas as the season goes along; perhaps now only brown is selling, while at Christmas, everyone will be wanting pink. In order to make clothes that can be worn everywhere, I'm using fabrics that work all year round, like jersey and heavy silk. And then I keep in close touch with what's selling and what's not selling; I talk with New York every day."

Versace's relationship with contemporary art had grown more intense than ever. At the first Arte/Moda Biennale at the Forte Belvedere in Florence, which created imaginative matches between artists and designers, Versace—paired with Roy Lichtenstein—designed a stunning red dress to go with the American pop artist's sculpture. And in the October issue of *Interview*—founded by Andy Warhol and edited by Ingrid Sischy—a number of artists, including Julian

Schnabel, Francesco Clemente, Frank Moore and the photographers Richard Avedon and Bruce Weber celebrated Versace's creative talent in a fifty-page supplement to the magazine titled "The Art of Being You" (Leonardo Arte published it as a book the following year).

Versace's passion for art was visible also in his spring-summer 1997 collection shown that fall. The striking items he sent out were inspired by his favorite artists: big red hearts following Jim Dine, the colors and shapes of Lichtenstein and Schnabel. The clothes were a great success with his clients and industry fashionistas. "The year 2000," predicted Versace, "will mark the triumph of femininity, free of all preconceptions. Women will want to amaze and amuse. That is why I came up with these 'arty' clothes, because today it is only art that amazes and amuses."

Business, meanwhile, was good. The Versace brand was expanding its collaboration with the Zegna group, and to the Versace Classic V2 line for men, begun in 1990, they now added a collection for women. This was a genuine prêt-à-porter line complete with accessories, intended primarily for the American and Asian markets and offering prices somewhat below Versace's other collections. The number of shops owned by Gianni Versace also continued to grow. "We're going to double them," Santo told *Il Sole 24 Ore*. "We intend to invest 150 billion lire in new stores. It's expensive, but we get a return."

Versace was ever more attached to America. And so it was there that he decided to celebrate his twentieth anniversary in the fashion business. "America brought me success," he told reporters. The stage, naturally, would be his corner of Manhattan. On October 23 he held a great housewarming party for his new town house on East 64th Street. Pop-rock playing in the background, the entire Versace family was there to greet the guests—hip New York society from Julian Schnabel to Woody Allen and James Ivory. The U.S. press looked on wide-eyed at the amazing opulence of Versace's residence, crowned with great quantities of modern and contemporary art. They counted eighteen Picassos spread among the various rooms, not to mention Warhols and Basquiats, enough to impress even the hard-to-please *New York Times*.

Two days later was the annual Versus show and then the opening of the gargantuan boutique on Fifth Avenue. *New Yorker* editor Tina Brown was in charge of the glamorous party. The press photos of the guests—Elton John and Bon Jovi at the piano before 750 select invitees—traveled around the world. *The New York Times* ran an article about the event headlined, "Lorenzo de Versace: Prince of Luxury," that compared the designer to Lorenzo de' Medici, noting that the company's sales amounted to $970 million a year. And Versace was invited to take part in the morning talk show *USA Today*—the first Italian designer to be invited on the show—where a crowd worthy of a football stadium paid tribute to him in the NBC studio.

The last landmark in that busy year was a book, titled *Rock and Royalty*, published in England by Abbeville Press. This coffe table book alternated portraits of the

English royal family with images shot by photographers like Avedon, Penn and Weber—images of people in various states of dress and undress. A small diplomatic incident would ensue. Princess Diana had agreed to write a preface for the book, but she incautiously neglected to see the layout pages before accepting. And so, after the first edition of the book came out in Italy with her accolade (Versace is "an esthete seeking the essence of beauty"), she withdrew her preface from the book. Her defection meant that the charity gala—planned for February 1997 in London timed to the British release of Versace book—would be annulled. Versace, who was by no means happy about it, neverthless guaranteed the sum he had hoped to collect in charity to the Elton John AIDS Foundation. He let it be known he was annoyed about the controversy surrounding his friend Diana's role in the book and canceled the benefit party to protect her. The princess and Gianni quickly overcame any bad feelings, and soon the designer would be sending her three new evening gowns.

But Versace had little to say back in Italy about his twenty-year anniversary celebrated in New York. He gave very few interviews. To *Corriere della Sera* he confided, "I'm very much influenced by technology and by the fabulous fabrics that we Italians are world leaders in manufacturing. I may be selling my clothes via Internet soon. On the personal side, I feel I've been reborn after my illness, just like in *Resurrection*, the painting presented to me by Sebastian Matta. I feel at peace now, very relaxed. I'm fortunate to have a wonderful family. At times we tear each other to pieces, but we always do it in order to create something. We have a pact in which we always reunite, here and now, together. Whatever happens."

CHAPTER 19
Suddenly

Versace's new orientation was clearly visible at his Atelier show on January 18, 1997, in Paris. The collection was dedicated to lightness and sobriety. "My whole collection should fit in a suitcase," he said. There was not a single suit, just little embroidered sweaters paired with skirts. And gossamer dresses of layers of organza and chiffon in pastel colors, with straps of Swarovsky crystal beads, and "hems finished by hand with tiny beads on the edge, like the head scarves Turkish women wear," as Versace said. There was also a tribute to modern art, with dresses inspired by Alexander Calder's mobiles. The supermodels had disappeared, either because they were engaged in more remunerative advertising contracts, like Kate Moss, or had new boyfriends, like Christy Turlington, but also because the times had changed. In their place, Versace engaged slender young models with less personality, apart from the aristocratic Stella Tennant, whom Gianni had been enamoured of for a while now, and newcomer Amy Wesson, discovered by Donatella. Only Naomi Campbell—casting fiery looks at her fiancé in the first row, dancer Joaquin Cortés—was still with Versace. In that week of Paris haute couture where the new names were John Galliano at Dior and Alexander McQueen at Givenchy, Versace was feeling confident. "There are two possible routes" for haute couture, he said. "The hyper-creative English make clothes that are suitable only to be photographed. Others combine imagination and actual exigencies. My way is the second way."

His show was a great success. In September, President Jacques Chirac had decided, Versace would be named Commendateur des Arts. And the evening before at Théâtre National de Chaillot, he had been acclaimed for the effortless costumes designed for Béjart's *Le presbytère n'a rien perdu de son charme*, an allegory about AIDS dedicated to the memory of Freddy Mercury and Jorge Donn with music by Mozart and Queen—a performance that ended, to much applause and more than a few tears, with a moving appearance by Elton John, singing *The Show Must Go On.*

The Milan shows for fall-winter 1997–1998 fashions also confirmed Versace's new direction. This time he showed only the Gianni Versace line; Istante and Versus were planned for a different venue. The Versace look was a long jacket that doubled as a dress. It was a dress cut—or cut out—to reveal the shoulders or the back. It dispensed with buttons altogether in favor of a clean, crisp line that managed to be both highly tailored and super-sexy. But now Versace had grown impatient with mere fashion shows. He told the press: "The era of the designer is over. The creator of fashion must return to the role of entrepreneur. I intend to appear less and work more."

"The traditional fashion show means nothing anymore," he said to *la Repubblica*. "We must create events. My menswear and a part of the womenswear that should appear on the runway in Milan in October, I plan to show in Florence during the preview of the Béjart ballet *Barocco—Bel Canto* dedicated to the marvelous castrato singers of the Baroque period, for which I've designed the costumes. The October show I plan to do in Washington at the White House, when President Clinton will be presenting me with an award. And who knows, I might decide to rent Madison Square Garden to show my clothes to the mass public in real time, that is, when the clothes are in the shops and not as we do now, six months in advance. I'm fed up with exposing my ideas and seeing them copied because of this perverse system we have that no longer meets the needs of the market."

As always Versace was looking ahead. Globalization was imposing new choices, and he had to ask himself, "And what if we can no longer provide a coherent image, what if we can no longer understand what people want?" At the same time, Gianni Versace S.p.A. was about to change its dimensions. "Right now I'm concentrating on transforming the Versace firm into a public company so that we can join the Milan Bourse next year. Our accounts have been consolidated since 1986; brand sales totaled 1.7 trillion lire in 1996; group sales totaled 845 billion lire." Versace's strategy was changing, CEO Santo Versace explained to Paola Bottelli in *Il Sole 24 Ore*. "For three seasons now we've been cutting our price lists, and by the end of the next season the average reduction will be around 15–20 percent. Let me be clear: this means without touching quality, merely taking advantage of the increase in volume and rationalizing our production plan." The price cut applied to all the collections. "Yes, because the consumers in all categories are changing," said Santo. "They have less money in many countries, including Italy. The money that was circulating in 1992, if all goes well, we'll see it again in five years. At the beginning of the nineties people bought things with their eyes and their heart; today they buy with their brains and their pocketbooks."

Santo also spoke about plans to list the company. "We had talked about doing so by the end of 1997 but now we're looking at listing the stock in Milan by June 1998. And we're also interested in Wall Street." Asked why they had delayed their entry on the Milan Bourse, Santo added, "We're now completing our corporate restructuring, which involves reducing the number of our companies and reordering our real estate exposure." The *Financial Times* observed that "Versace, with direct and indirect turnover of 1.5 trillion lire and a further increase in sales last year, could prove an excellent investment." John Fairchild, publisher of *WWD* and *W*, also had good things to say about the group when he lunched with Gianni at Via Gesù. "You're increasingly becoming a major brand," he told him. Gianni was delighted. "Yes, I was pleased," he told *Panorama*. "Because Fairchild doesn't pay compliments lightly, and above all because nobody has his finger on the pulse of fashion worldwide the way he does. Of course I'll continue to be the designer at Versace, but I'm going to have more and more obligations to my clients, and when we go public, to the investors who buy stock in our company."

At the end of April, *Il Sole 24 Ore* reported, Versace gave Barclays investment arm, Barclays de Zoete Wedd, a mandate to bring together a pool of banks to finance the company. "The three-year loan, for a total of 100 billion lire, will be underwritten by a restricted group of financial institutions," the paper reported.

The surprise that Versace had pre-announced came on June 25. At the 52nd presentation of Pitti Immagine in Florence, Versace showed his summer menswear collection. His stage set was the Boboli Gardens where Maurice Béjart was putting on his ballet *Barocco—Bel Canto*. Forty dancers from the Béjart Ballet Lausanne wearing the simple costumes designed by Versace, would move about among the models wearing the designer's summer collection, very restrained, almost minimalist clothes. Then, a further surprise: Naomi Campbell appeared on the stage to show off three dresses from the Atelier collection, dresses that would be seen on the runway a few days later in Paris. Naomi held a pistol in hand and she fired it at the audience, brusquely interrupting the harmony of the music by Handel, Broschi and Salazar, the dancers and the scene. The 1,000 guests—journalists, big buyers, Florentine aristocrats, leading names in fashion from Ferragamo to Marzotto and Zegna, stars of the art and movie worlds like Julian Schnabel and Dennis Hopper—froze, bewildered. The pause lasted only an instant, like a passing cloud which then dispersed. The evening proved a great success, and the reception at the Boboli gardens went off beautifully. Versace, Béjart and a few others had a light supper at midnight at the home of the Marchese and Marchesa Antinori. The following day Béjart received the Arte e Moda prize from the city of Florence and Versace was awarded the Pitti Immagine Uomo 1997 prize.

The evening of June 26 Versace travelled to the Ravenna Festival on the Adriatic for the first night of Béjart's ballet *Messe pour le temps présent* at the Teatro Astoria—costumes by Versace. Mario Pasi remembers their dinner after the performance well. "We were sitting at the same table with Béjart, Versace and I. And when Versace mentioned he was about to leave for Miami, Béjart said to him, 'Stay here, Gianni, it's better.' Versace replied, 'No, I have to go, but when I come back we'll have a big party at my house.' And he turned to me: 'Pasi, bring your wife.' I can't get the image of that evening out of my mind. In pictures Béjart and I looked smiling and cheerful, but Versace had a sad expression, and it struck me."

Naomi Campbell once again starred at the Paris haute couture shows, which opened, as usual, with Versace's show on July 6. She played Byzantine Empress Theodora, wife of 6th-century emperor Justinian, as seen by Versace, who had fallen in love with the Byzantine mosaics in the Ravenna church of Sant'Apollinaire in Classe, and who had recreated their allure in a matchless metal mesh fabric woven with Byzantine crosses. *WWD*, in an article headlined, "Vamp It Up," wrote: "Versace dared his audience to react. Love it or hate it, but check your indifference at the door."

Versace was charged up and full of projects. Andrea Tremolada recalls, with some emotion, an evening they spent together in April on their return from the Cosmoprof beauty fair in Bologna where a Versace fragrance had won a prize. "We were at the Hotel Baglioni bar. We talked about what we were working on and about the company's upcoming listing on the Milan Bourse. Gianni said to me: 'What I've done in these first twenty years is nothing compared to what we're going to do in the next ten.' " Tremolada went on: "Gianni was a very generous man. If he were to read in the *Corriere della Sera* that somebody was ill, or if he learned that one of his employees had some ailment, he would send his own doctors and make anonymous contributions." Gianni Versace loved people and he loved life. Tremolada recalls another episode that took place in Miami in April. "I was there, too, as Gianni's guest, and it was my birthday. He said to me: 'I'm inviting you to lunch at Caffè Milano, bring your friends.' When we stepped out of his house on Ocean Drive, while the gate was opening, I saw a mob of people with cameras hunkered down on the other side of the street. I was embarrassed and little bit nervous. But Gianni was a star. I asked him: 'But don't you ever worry that someone might do you harm?' He didn't have any bodyguards, he just walked around alone at all hours of the day—he had remained himself, very casual. And he said: 'I've never harmed anyone and I don't see why anyone would want to harm me.' "

On the morning of July 15, 1997, Gianni Versace walked out of Casa Casuarina quite early in the morning, as he always did, to get the papers at the News Café. He and Antonio D'Amico had been in Miami for a few days for the brief break they liked to take in July after the Atelier show in Paris. Here's how D'Amico remembers it: "I woke up at seven-fifteen because at eight a.m. I was expecting Lazaro, a Cuban friend who was supposed to come to play tennis. I got dressed and went downstairs for breakfast. I asked the staff: Is Mr. Versace already in the pool? He went out to buy the newspapers, they told me. Meanwhile Lazaro had arrived. We're drinking coffee when I hear two shots, far away, from the direction of the street. I get up and look out the windows of the dining room, and I see the front gate is open. I run out, followed by Lazaro, and see Gianni lying on the steps in a pool of blood. Then my vision clouds up, a scream bursts from my lips, and I feel like I'm going to keel over. I raise my eyes and I see a man watching us from the sidewalk. Run after him, I say to Lazaro. The man turns toward Lazaro and points his gun at him, then he starts running toward a multilevel parking garage. There's a police officer a little way down the street, and Lazaro runs up to him and tells him what happened. But the murderer has already disappeared without a trace. Then the cops show up, and so does the ambulance that will take Gianni to the hospital. They won't let me go with him; they say I have to stay at the scene of the crime because I'm a witness. I'm there in the house for two hours with Lazaro and the staff. A detective arrives and he asks me to give him a detailed reconstruction of Versace's last moments. Then the cops come back and I go with them, along with Lazaro and the butler, to the police station. The questions begin. I answer fully and to the best of my knowledge. They show me photos of the presumed murderer. I have no idea who he is. In every picture he looks completely different: one time he has a beard, one time his hair is dyed. In one picture, however, I see that he looks like the man I saw on the sidewalk. They keep me there until ten p.m. Then the owner of the Versace boutique in Miami comes to pick me up and take me back to Casa Casuarina."

Rody Mirri's book *It's Your Song* published by Vannini Editrice, recounts the long love story between Gianni Versace and Antonio D'Amico, and tells what happened next. "Santo and Donatella were in Rome to present their show at Piazza di Spagna—it was cancelled when news of the tragedy reached the other side of the Atlantic. The fashion world was in mourning. The next morning they arrived in Miami on a private plane along with Emanuela, the head of the press office. It was only at about five p.m. that they got permission, along with Antonio, to see the body in the hospital's mortuary chapel. The gunshots had partially disfigured Gianni's face, but kindly expert hands had restored his appearance. There was a commemoration, the cremation ceremony, and Antonio found himself on the private plane with Donatella, Santo and Emanuela. Few words were spoken, many tears were shed. In Santo's lap was a brass urn with Gianni's ashes. D'Amico thought about how this would be his last flight. They took the urn to the cemetery in Moltrasio where Gianni wanted to be buried on the tranquil shores of Lake Como. A family from the town offered them a temporary space in their private chapel."

Gianni Versace's murderer was Andrew Phillip Cunanan, 27, a gigolo and "high end gay prostitute," as his own mother described him. A serial killer, he had been on the FBI's 10 Most Wanted List from May 12. But the FBI had been aware of him before that, ever since, on April 29, he had killed 28-year-old Jeffrey Trail, a boyfriend, with a hammer, wrote reporter Leonardo Coen in *la Repubblica*. Trail's body was found rolled up in a carpet in the home of another of Cunanan's lovers, David Madson, 33. Madson was found dead on May 3, a gunshot wound to the temple. His body lay abandoned on the shores of a lake near Minneapolis. Madson's red Jeep Cherokee had disappeared. On May 4 in Chicago, Lee Miglin, 72, a multi-millionaire real estate developer who rewarded his lovers with lavish sums, was also found murdered. Cunanan had slashed his throat with a pair of scissors and a saw blade. Madson's Jeep was found nearby, but Miglin's car had disappeared. Cunanan drove it to New Jersey. On May 9 he was in Pennsville, New Jersey, where he shot William Reese, a cemetery caretaker, dead. Nearby, police found Miglin's Lexus, the latest in a series of macabre execution clues left by Cunanan—who was then off to Florida, to Miami.

"Cunanan," wrote Leonardo Coen, "was now planning the hit that would project him into the Olympus of criminal notoriety. Versace was an easy target, a stunning celebrity hit. Cunanan would be as unforgettable as the greatest of all bad guys." Cunanan killed himself with his pistol on July 23 in a house boat anchored at Miami Beach. "The suicide—so the death was defined in the police record—took place however with a timing that left a lot of room for doubt," wrote Coen. " 'Rather than turn himself in, he's going to kill himself,' an FBI profiler had predicted of the serial killer while he was on the run. Andrew Phillip Cunanan died with his secrets. And with his motives. The silence of the guilty is convenient for everyone. It's convenient for the politicians worried about their city's image problem and a possible collapse in that indispensable resource, tourism. It's convenient for the FBI and the Miami Beach police, who have been accused of being less than efficient for allowing one of America's most wanted men to escape—three times."

People were in shock. The fashion world was in mourning. Santo and Donatella Versace got Don Bartolomeo, the parish priest of Moltrasio and a family friend, to bless Gianni's ashes. Donatella's children, Allegra and Daniel, and Santo's children, Antonio and Francesca, all of them very close to their uncle, attended the ceremony in tears. The Versace family also carrried the urn to Via Gesù in Milan, so that friends could pay their respects. There were many of us who went there—many, many, from the world of fashion. None of us could believe what had happened. We all felt we must say our last goodbyes to Gianni Versace there where he had worked, where he created his splendid clothes and the magic of his unforgettable fashion shows, before the public ceremony, which would be a more solemn occasion but inevitably also more of a celebrity affair.

The family asked Barbara Vitti, Milan's top public relations person for fashion, to take charge of the public ceremony. "In those days I had my own company," Vitti recalls. "For Versace, I took care of cultural events like the Avedon show at Palazzo Reale in 1995. When they called to tell me about Gianni's death, I fainted. Gianni was so alive, so generous, so wonderful. And I was immensely sorry for Santo and Donatella. I went over there right away, to help out in their press office with the thousands of phone calls that were pouring in. Speaking to me from Miami they said it would be nice to have a funeral mass for Gianni in the Duomo. I agreed right away to help out. I thought about how many people would want to participate and then I asked Leonardo Mondadori to go with me to meet the mayor, Gabriele Albertini. Then I went to the Duomo to meet Don Gianni Zappa of the archdiocese curia, who told me that the mass would be celebrated by Msgr. Angelo Majo, archpriest of the Duomo of Milan. I got him to give me a copy of the sermon to send to Maurice Béjart, who was supposed to read it. In the meantime, Santo, Donatella and Emanuela had returned to Milan. I went to see them to bring them up to date. Then I telephoned Luciano Migliavacca, conductor and master of the choir at the Duomo to let him know that two 'opera singers,' Sting and Elton John, would sing *The Lord Is My Shepherd*. I remember that Msgr. Migliavacca was taken somewhat ill and I had to sing him the melody myself over the phone. That little episode even managed to get a smile out of Santo and Donatella. Msgr. Migliavacca would later tell the *Corriere della Sera*, 'I'd let them sing again, if the circumstances came about. It was a beautiful encounter between the liturgy and a secular sensibility.' Flowers, masses of flowers, kept arriving. I suggested they advise, in the death notice in *Corriere della Sera*, that those who wished could instead send a contribution to the Italian Association for Cancer Research. Santo and Donatella agreed immediately. Then Emanuela Schmeidler and I planned where to seat the guests who would arrive for the mass in the Duomo. In the front row, the family with Antonio D'Amico, Elton John and David Furnish, Princess Diana, Béjart, Sting and his wife Trudie.... Just behind, Karl Lagerfeld, Anna Wintour, Naomi Campbell.... The Versace family gave a generous offering to the Duomo and we sent a letter of thanks to Cardinal Martini, then archbishop of Milan."

Gianni Versace's funeral mass was celebrated in the Duomo at six p.m. on July 22, in front of 5,000 mourners. "Princesses, models, singers, actresses, athletes, fashion editors, designers, choreographers, the great international stars of the nineties...came from around the world for the final society salute to one of them, for one *like* them—a celebrity, a man of wealth and luxury, of the wild and good life, a creator of style for the elect and of dreams for the masses," wrote Natalia Aspesi in *la Repubblica*. "But in the sedate silence of the cathedral, the emotion, the grief, the reddened faces and the tears are real.... They are crying for him, for Gianni Versace, and crying for themselves, for all the marvelous, the thrilling, the unique things that they have shared, with levity and with luck:

parties and love affairs, adventures and talent, show business and desire, creativity and a way of life, fame and beauty, gorgeous houses and travel, the certainty they have the best of life and are deservedly loved by the rest of the world.

"This is an act of faith, not a performance, says the priest who is celebrating the mass and who legitimates the grief that bows sister Donatella and brother Santo, but not that of Antonio, the companion of a lifetime, the one most wounded, most lost. And even the people behind the police lines, and those who were able to squeeze into the Duomo, understand that they are not a 'public,' a bunch of fans come to see the latest display of stars, this time stars in mourning, but a multitude wishing to participate in a dramatic occasion that in some way will deprive them too of a piece of a dream, of a notion of beauty. And this is why few who regard it as inappropriate that the solemn Duomo should host a designer's funeral mass—one whom the more fastidious might judge too much a symbol of frivolity, of waste, of erotic temptation, of a way of life that didn't suit a believer. The Duomo has seen the funerals of the victims of terrorist bombings like that of Piazza Fontana or Via Palestro[1] but also the last rites of Puccini, Toscanini and Eugenio Montale—a great composer, a great conductor and a great poet. Now at the end of the nineties, the city is mourning for one of the greats of today: a

---

1. Piazza Fontana: in 1969 a right-wing terrorist bomb killed seventeen inside a bank in that Milan square. Via Palestro: in 1993, Mafia exponents set off a bomb in this Milan street, killing five.

fashion designer, a legend who seemed untouchable and who instead was murdered as happens today, out of madness or rage, by chance or on commission, by an everyday killer, cold and probably unknown to his victim."

In mid-September, Santo and Donatella with her husband, Paul Beck, and Antonio D'Amico assembled at the Milanese office of notary Luciano Severini in Piazza San Babila for the reading of Gianni Versace's will. Versace named Donatella's daughter Allegra, eleven years old, his sole heir, leaving her his 50 percent share of the business. He left his collection of Picassos to her younger brother, Daniel. Antonio D'Amico got a life annuity of 50 million lire per month and use-rights to all of Versace's houses during his lifetime.

Today, eleven years after his death, tracing the extraordinary path followed by Gianni Versace, speaking with those who knew him and worked with him, I found that his memory is very much alive everywhere; the remorse, profound; the emotion, sincere. Feelings I share when I think of that brilliant creator of fashion and that gracious and sympathetic person whom I was lucky to know. Among the tributes, there is one published recently by the writer and designer Quirino Conti in *Corriere della Sera*. It is titled, "Gianni, Dionysus Lost."

"It was just an ordinary day. Routine, as is always true for a day predestined to leave its mark on the spirit and on time. Meanwhile the news bounced from one end of the world to the other, frenetic and intolerable. Never had fashion been so touched to the quick, and by such terrible grief. The usual, habitual words, no matter how strongly felt, suddenly seem inappropriate. Impertinent. Vain and ambiguous. Dionysus had abandoned his temple. Violently. And a terrifying silence had now descended over all. Just as the cicada falls silent at nightfall, in one second the deafening sound of the harpsichord, the horns, the brasses and the drums had been silenced. The most sensual of rhythms heard in the language of our modernity.

"Many, many things were said. Except, perhaps, for one. That with the death of Gianni Versace, the era of style came to an end, and nothing would serve—new all-purpose company chiefs, little swarms of designers, all kinds of management—to bring it back to life. Just as for that poor tortured body. Because history is constantly revealing itself in metaphors. To read and interpet. And for fashion, it was in that post-modern Babylon that Miami was then, that history would be fulfilled. While the inebriating vitality of that hybrid and metamorphic god was draining out. Taking, just as a true master of style must, everyone and everything with him. Mounted on a panther, forcing its pace, he led the loud and festive march of the god of instinct and the night. He arrived in Milan with the feverish determination of those who come from far, far away. Already knowing the price and the weight of prejudice and the forbidden. And yet, with the wild levity belonging to that ancient cult whose unmistakable signs he wore on his face, the whole world opened up before him as he came through....

"But what was most striking about him was his absolute lack of doubt. And his vitality. So much so that his new way of sketching out his own, autonomous style, was almost more present in his gaze—dark, rapid and resolute, his expression ever so concentrated—than in the subsequent objective working out of it. His energy was tireless, unquiet and as he said right off, modern. But Milan seemed destined to be ruled by another pretender. As if between him—Giorgio Armani—between this city and a new style, there was a predestined preference for the first-born. And so it was. At least until Versace took the crown and reigned. Founding a diarchy. Or better, to match the spirit of those times, a double empire. And nothing could stop his ascent, so intimidating in the way it posed profound esthetic-sociological questions. The world lined up behind him. So that he—the outsider, the exotic one, the stranger—became this city, its style and its unforgettable master. In fact everything in that fatal decade was changing, and a new era, with a new audience, demanded a role, a status and a form. And Versace would cast that form onto a new society that, everywhere, was shaping itself around an astonishing vitality and an easy arousal never before dreamed of. He being the clever, lucid, conscious salesman. He who, like a tamer of wild beasts, contained style (or perhaps the fragmentation of styles) when style was crumbling in a world that had become difficult to decipher, and could not bear the weight of tradition and the work of creating a single, complex language.

"And so it was he, out of elective affinity, who took on the job—the weighty job—of making levity legitimate.... And meanwhile fashion, behind everyone's back, had decided to change tack, or rather, to change its nature. And following that terrible July 15, 1997, for a long time there was nothing but emptiness and creative regret.... And that regret, mixed with remorse, imposed a long, formal mourning. A huge, official *mea culpa*.... And afterwards, there were only followers, of various levels of talent.... But none of them had the instinctual wildness of the prototype. Not even the clothes that had more or less come back to life. Because it was from the god's gaze that the world drew energy. Intoxication and legitimacy. Otherwise style, and fashion itself, must disappear. And post-fashion was to be as antithetical as could be imagined to that effervescent talent—it would be difficult, unpleasant and conceptual. We can only imagine how he would have laughed at it, maybe tempered it and corrected it. So hungry, omnivorous, so great a popularizer, Versace."

Alessi, Roberto, ed. *Versace, eleganza di vita.* Milan: Rusconi, 1990.

Avedon, Richard. *Woman in the Mirror.* New York: Harry N. Abrams/The Richard Avedon Foundation, 2005.

Avedon, Richard (photographs), and Truman Capote (comments). *Observations.* Lucerne/New York: Camera Publishers in collaboration with Simon and Schuster, 1959.

Bocca, Nicoletta, and Chiara Buss, eds. *Gianni Versace, l'abito per pensare.* Milan: Arnoldo Mondadori Editore Arte, 1989.

Borioli, Gisella. *10 anni di moda: 1980–1990.* Milan: Edimoda, 1990.

Buss, Chiara, and Richard Martin, eds. *Gianni Versace.* Milan: Leonardo Arte, 1998.

Frisa, Maria Luisa, and Stefano Tonchi, eds. *Excess: moda e underground negli anni '80.* Milan: Charta, 2004.

Giacomoni, Silvia. *L'Italia della moda.* Milan: Mazzotta, 1984.

Guarino, Mario. *Versace versus Versace.* Rome: Fabio Croce Editore, 2003.

Laurenzi, Laura. *Liberi di amare.* Milan: Rizzoli, 2006.

Martin, Richard. *Gianni Versace.* New York: The Metropolitan Museum of Art, 1997.
Mirri, Rody. *It's Your Song.* Gussago: Vannini Editrice, 2007.
Mulassano, Adriana. *I mass-moda.* Florence: Edizioni G. Spinelli & C., 1979.

Pasi, Mario, ed. *Versace Teatro*, volume I (English/Italian). Milan: Franco Maria Ricci, 1987.

Seeling, Charlotte. *Fashion: The Century of the Designer, 1900–1999.* Cologne: Konemann, 2000.
Strong, Roy, ed. *Versace Teatro*, volume II (English/Italian). Milan: Franco Maria Ricci, 1992.

Vergani, Guido. *La Sala Bianca: nascita della moda italiana.* Milan: Electa, 1992.
Vergani, Guido, ed. *Fashion Dictionary.* New York: Baldini Castoldi Dalai, 2006.
Versace, Gianni. *Do Not Disturb.* New York: Abbeville Press, 1996.
Versace, Gianni. *Men Without Ties.* New York: Abbeville Press, 1994.
Versace, Gianni. *Ricami e decori, decori e ricami.* Milan: Leonardo, 1993.

Versace, Gianni, and Omar Calabrese. *Vanitas, lo stile dei sensi.* Milan: Leonardo, 1991.

Versace, Gianni, and Omar Calabrese. *Versace Signatures.* Rome: Leonardo-De Luca Editori, 1992.

Versace, Gianni, Germano Celant, Ingrid Sischy, and Richard Martin. *The Art of Being You.* New York: Abbeville Press, 1998.

Versace, Gianni, Lady Julia Trevelyan Oman, Hamish Bowles, and Isabella Bossi Fedrigotti. *Vanitas: Designs.* New York: Abbeville Press, 1994.

Versace, Gianni, and Donatella Versace. *South Beach Stories.* Milan: Leonardo Arte, 1993.

Versace, Gianni, Princess Diana of Wales, Elton John, and Donatella Versace. *Rock and Royalty.* New York: Abbeville Press, 1997.

Also in Baldini Castoldi Dalai *editore* Inc.'s list:

Fashion Dictionary edited by Guido Vergani

Being Armani – A Biography by Renata Molho

I Kill by Giorgio Faletti

Next to be released:

Cityscapes by Gabriele Basilico, Fall 2008

Beirut 1991(2003) by Gabriele Basilico, Fall 2008

Brunello, Montalcino and I – The Prince of Wines' true story by Ezio Rivella, Spring 2009